BORN DEAD—DIE ALIVE

Cultivating a Humane Humanity with Technology

SALMA NOUN

For more information, email salmanoun@gmail.com.

ISBN: 979-8-89316-867-9 (paperback)
ISBN: 979-8-89316-868-6 (hardcover)
ISBN: 979-8-89316-866-2 (eBook)

LET'S CONNECT

Visit my website and follow me on your favorite social media sites for the latest technology updates, exclusive interviews, podcasts and more.

salmanoun.com

*To my husband, Youssef, my best friend, incredible coach,
and biggest supporter—you inspire me to be better, challenge
me to dream bigger, and remind me that anything is
possible. Thank you for always being in my corner.*

*To our tiny miracle, Lilia—and to all future generations—may you dream
fearlessly, harness the boundless possibilities of technology, and weave it
into a tapestry of more intelligent, compassionate, and human world.*

Technology is a gift of God. After the gift of life it is perhaps the greatest of God's gifts. It is the mother of civilizations, of arts and of science.

—Freeman Dyson,
theoretical physicist and mathematician

TABLE OF CONTENTS

INTRODUCTION—THE QUEST BEGINS

M y journey into understanding life's deeper meanings began early. At just four years old, I asked my mom, "Where is Grandpa? Why have I never seen him?"

Her eyes shimmered with a sadness I couldn't understand as she softly said, "He's in the clouds."

I further questioned, "Can I call him?"

A single tear slipped from her eye as she tenderly clarified that death is a final state; once someone has passed, they cease to exist in this world, and communication is no longer possible.

My mother's explanation of his presence "in the clouds" and the permanence of death planted the seeds in me of a lifelong quest to understand the boundaries of existence. This curiosity burgeoned as I grew, leading me down a path filled with philosophical inquiries and existential reflections, all while navigating the expectations and norms of a conventional life.

When I realized that life has a lot of boundaries, that there are mysteries beyond our understanding, forces that we cannot control, it both fascinated and frightened me. I felt small, confined by the expectations and routines society expects of us, like following a path that's already been laid out—school, work, and the cycle continues.

Despite academic success and societal acceptance, I felt a profound sense of disconnect and disagreement. The traditional paths of education and career, even in the field of engineering, which I had chosen, seemed to offer little in the way of understanding the deeper mysteries and questions that intrigued me. This feeling of being out of step grew as I became more disillusioned with the educational system, recognizing that many people's career choices were motivated more by necessity than by true passion. This sparked in me a curiosity that would only grow stronger with time.

School served at least as a fertile ground for nurturing my philosophical interests. My inclination towards philosophy was met with encouragement, especially from teachers who were often impressed by the depth and insight of my essays and ideas.

Among those who recognized my passion for exploring life's mysteries, in addition to my husband and family, was my friend Ghita B. She was more than just a friend; she was my journey's companion, always ready to listen and engage with my latest philosophical ideas and existential questions. Our discussions spanned hours, diving into topics that most found too daunting or abstract to consider. It was with Ghita's encouragement that I began to explore philosophy more deeply, seeking answers to questions that have puzzled humans for millennia.

In 2017, while in Paris, my philosophical journey took a significant turn. I began a research project exploring the nature of death, the possibilities of life beyond, and the intersections of philosophical, religious, and scientific perspectives on these questions. German philosopher Gottfried Leibnitz's theory of monads and philosophical thoughts became a key focus of my analysis, offering a framework to ponder the complexities of existence and the universe.

Every person has a life full of unique thoughts, feelings, and experiences. It's a terrible loss when these disappear, both for the person and for everyone around them. This makes me believe science might have the answers. Like scientists studying the universe or philosophers pondering what it means to exist, I want to understand life, death, and what comes after.

This period was marked by intense exploration. However, personal reasons led me to pause this deep research though the questions and curiosity never left me.

BRIDGING PHILOSOPHY AND TECHNOLOGY

My entry into the professional world marked a new phase in my journey, where my philosophical inclinations met the pragmatic world of technology. Working in this field, I encountered an ever-expanding universe of tech-related subjects. With an engineer's mindset, I naturally began to draw connections between technology, science, and philosophy.

This blend of interests led me to delve into the emerging realms of technology and innovations. While I found many of the use cases fascinating, I couldn't help but notice a recurring theme: a heavy orientation towards business, profit-making, and entertainment. It seemed as though the potential of these technologies to serve humanity, particularly in fields like education, research, and healthcare, was often neglected in favor of more superficial digital applications. This realization was both a disappointment and a call to action. The predominant focus on using breakthroughs simply to entertain and make profit, rather than to fundamentally improve human conditions, underscored a misalignment with my vision of technology as a force for good.

Amidst this world of rapid technological progress, my philosophical reflections gained a new perspective.

Like American civil rights leader Martin Luther King Jr., I have a dream: to extend the human lifespan. Not merely making small improvements to our health and lifespan. This dream is grounded in the real possibilities that technology offers for pushing beyond our biological boundaries. This vision is not founded on hope alone but on the tangible innovations being made in fields such as genomics, biotechnology, and artificial intelligence. These areas, when directed with a purpose that transcends commercial interests, hold the key to redefining human existence.

"BORN DEAD, DIE ALIVE": A CALL TO REIMAGINE OUR DESTINY

This book, *Born Dead, Die Alive*, is a culmination of these reflections and revelations. It is a narrative that challenges us to look beyond the conventional applications of technology, to envision a world where our collective ingenuity is harnessed for the profoundest of all causes: the enrichment of human life itself. Through this work, I aim to bridge the gap between the philosophical questions that have haunted humanity since time immemorial and the technological advancements that offer us unprecedented opportunities for transformation.

In crafting *Born Dead, Die Alive*, my intention goes beyond merely discussing the transformative era of technology. It tackles how AI and advanced computing might unlock a kind of Universal Intelligence—transcending the limitations of human cognition, offering insights into realms that we, with our biological constraints, have been unable to penetrate. It also tackles how the evolution of AI and related technologies could transcend the mere augmentation of human capabilities, potentially reshaping our fundamental understanding of existence itself.

This book serves as a platform to argue for a significant shift in how we approach our technological advancements. It illuminates the concept of rebirth through technology, proposing that we can adopt new identities and lead new lives in a digital realm.

The narrative calls for a focus on technological developments that do more than entertain or offer superficial benefits. Instead, it advocates for innovations that fundamentally improve the human condition—by extending our lifespans and enhancing the quality of our lives. *Born Dead, Die Alive* challenges us to reconsider what it means to lead a fulfilling life, unveiling the journey of a society metaphorically "born dead," constrained within the confines of a system that fails to evolve. Yet, it envisions a hopeful future for subsequent generations. This future offers not just the chance to live fully, but also the possibility to "die alive." This metaphor signifies a life that transcends the limitations of our physical existence. Technological advancements can bridge the gap between our finite lives and the boundless potential of the human mind. Imagine exploring the universe, curing diseases, or even extending human lifespans—all within the realm of possibility.

As will be discussed in Chapter 12 "Is Singularity Near?" it's about how we can use technology to expand our abilities and presence, even beyond our physical existence. However, this transformation demands significant shifts in mentality, societal attitudes, and government investments in education, healthcare, and innovation. In this envisioned future, the saying, "Your grandpa is in the 'clouds'" could take on a literal meaning. Similar to the concept of Death 2.0 discussed in Chapter 11 "Death 2.0: Can We Live Forever," which proposes uploading and storing a person's thoughts and memories in a digital repository, like the cloud storage, for potential preservation after death so that those living can continue interacting with them in a meaningful way, even after they're gone.

My research is deeply rooted in the works of visionaries and scientists like Ray Kurzweil, notably drawing from his book *The Singularity Is Near,*[1] insights from *The Second Machine Age* by Erik Brynjolfsson and Andrew McAfee,[2] and explorations of Aaron Garrison's essay, "Mind, Machine, and the Empathic Revolution."[3] enabling a robust discussion on the pivotal role of technology in reshaping our future, promising a narrative that not only reflects on technological potential but also challenges us to imagine the vast possibilities for human progress.

Aligning perfectly with my mission to empower individuals through the positive potential of technology, I aim to dispel the prevailing negative mindset and the pervasive skepticism that technology will bring only destruction and disconnection. Instead, I want to show how technology can enhance our lives, lead to longevity, and foster a deeper sense of connection. By challenging misconceptions and dispelling societal myths, I aspire to inspire readers to harness the transformative power of technology for personal growth, meaningful relationships, and a brighter future. Ultimately, my big aim is to instill hope, optimism, and a proactive mindset toward technology's role in shaping our lives.

THE CLICK THAT SHAPED US: SOCIETY, SYSTEMS, AND THE DIGITAL SHIFT

PART 1

Part 1 examines how we can break free from a path where hidden agendas subtly dictate our future, leaving us feeling "born dead." Can we instead wrest control, actively shaping technology with the goal of "dying alive"—continuously striving for human betterment? Through examining hidden agendas, envisioning bold new models, redefining what progress means, and demystifying algorithms that control our potential, we'll chart a course where technology facilitates human flourishing.

In Chapter 1, we'll delve into the hidden individuals, systems, and agendas influencing which innovations flourish and which fade into obscurity. We'll challenge the idea that technology is inevitable, exploring how decisions made behind the scenes impact everything from our daily interactions to the fabric of our economies.

In Chapter 2, we'll envision a "model city" where policymakers and innovators experiment with new systems for education, jobs, and technology integration. This visionary approach has the potential to showcase what's truly possible, revealing new forms of work and business that we can't even fathom today.

Chapter 3 challenges us to think beyond traditional success metrics. Technological advancement unfolds gradually, with smaller innovations paving the way for breakthroughs, like the evolution from landlines to global video calls. Our history is filled with yesterday's "impossible" dreams becoming today's reality. Embracing the spirit of Arthur C. Clarke—that advanced technology is akin to magic—we need to question the limits we place on ourselves and consider new ways to measure societal success.

Finally, Chapter 4 tackles the subtle power of algorithms. While algorithms can certainly be helpful, it's crucial to become informed about algorithms and manage our digital footprint to safeguard privacy and autonomy. This chapter also focuses on the negative impacts algorithms have on our mental health and actions we can take to shape a digital world that both serves our needs and respects our well-being.

TECHNOLOGY'S DANCE: DIRECTED BY SOCIETY, POLITICS, AND ECONOMY

Everything is determined, the beginning as well as the end, by forces over which we have no control. It is determined for the insect as well as for the star. Human beings, vegetables or cosmic dust, we all dance to a mysterious tune, intoned in the distance by an invisible player.

—Albert Einstein

E verything is decided from the start, even the end. We all have no control over it, from tiny bugs to giant stars. We're all just moving to a strange song, played by a hidden musician far away. These words of Albert Einstein, long echoing through history, take on new meaning in the relentless march of digital transformation. As I watch technology race forward so fast, these words make me wonder: is this technological evolution already mapped out, a script we unknowingly follow? Do invisible algorithms subtly guide our online choices? Or are powerful corporations the true conductors, dictating the pace of change? Or maybe some unseen coalition of powerful figures are pulling the levers of this digital revolution?

Perhaps, like Einstein contemplating the grand design of the universe, we are simply awestruck observers, witnessing a dance of exponential progress where individual agency and technological forces intertwine. But a question lingers: who are these forces? Who are the unseen architects behind this relentless transformation?

The curiosity was partly sparked by the permeating presence of a vague "they" in overheard conversations with friends and family. "They have developed this," "They are introducing that," "They have decided," "They are controlling technology"—this nebulous "they" seemed to be at the helm, steering us through waves of innovation, decisions, and societal shifts.

But who are "THEY"?

My thoughts shifted between naive belief and skepticism. Was there a group, an entity, a consortium that decided which technological seeds would be released and which inventions would be hidden from the public eye? Was there a mysterious conclave deciding which advancements were allowed, determining which innovations were permitted to embed themselves within our societal fabric? These questions, born from youthful wonder, inspired me to write this chapter to provide answers for others with similar queries.

As we delve into this chapter, we aim to uncover the hidden influences shaping our digital world. We'll look at the individuals and systems quietly pulling the strings—and how society, the economy, and politics play a part in this story.

Together, we'll explore how these forces shape technology, examining their motives and the ethical questions they raise. This journey will take us beyond the familiar tech headlines and into the background where decisions are made, inventions succeed or fail, and the future is silently architected by the unseen hands of "THEY."

SOCIETY'S ROLE IN SHAPING TECHNOLOGY AND VICE VERSA
The Public's Acceptance or Resistance

It's often said that technology is only as effective as its user base. Human acceptance and resistance to new technologies can be seen as a reflection of societal values, beliefs, and even fears. Technology's success depends on people. History shows us this repeatedly. The Luddite movement in the 19th century saw workers destroying machines they feared would cost them their jobs. Another example that underscores this point is the initial reluctance to adopt calculators, especially in educational settings. When calculators were introduced, they faced resistance from educators and parents. The prevailing concern was that these devices would weaken basic arithmetic skills among students. Many believed that mastery over manual methods of computation should come first before introducing electronic aids. It wasn't just about a technological tool; it was about the societal emphasis on foundational learning and the perceived threat technology might pose to that.

Using the lens of the social construction of technology (SCOT) theory, we can argue that technological advancements don't just "happen." Instead, they're shaped by societal groups—companies, users, governments—their choices and their actions. SCOT posits that the ultimate form of a technology is influenced by the interpretations and priorities of various social groups. Thus, if a segment of society opposes or is skeptical about a particular technology, its widespread adoption and eventual design might be influenced or even compromised.

Cultural and societal norms heavily influence technological adoption. In some cultures, drones delivering goods might be seen as a convenience while in others, it's perceived as an invasion of privacy. The acceptance of telemedicine, especially mental health consultations, varies based on societal stigmas attached to medical care or therapy. The way society values privacy determines the acceptance and success of tracking apps or technologies. Society's trust or mistrust in technology, often rooted in cultural narratives or historical events, can significantly sway the trajectory of tech advancements. For instance, in Japan, robots are increasingly seen as potential companions or caregivers, rooted in cultural narratives that often portray robots in a positive light. In contrast, Western dystopian views might resist such integration.

In today's rapidly evolving technological landscape, Marshall McLuhan's theory of "the medium is the message" rings true more than ever. According to McLuhan, every medium embeds itself in any message it transmits, influencing how the message is perceived. In the context of the Digital Age, the internet isn't just a tool; it dictates the narrative, shapes perceptions, and even influences emotions. So, if you are fine with the narrative and emotions, then you will adopt it easily. Consequently, if the societal consensus aligns with these narratives and emotional resonances, technological adoption becomes frictionless. But when adoption is effortless, are we being critical enough of the technologies we embrace?

In contemporary times, society's apprehensions toward technology have evolved but not disappeared. The techno-skeptical rhetoric of the past, as seen with the Luddites or the calculator debate, has transformed, echoing today's concerns about data privacy, state surveillance, and environmental degradation.

For instance, the ongoing discussions about the "metaverse," a potential next version of the internet where our online and offline lives increasingly blend, raise questions about data privacy, personal autonomy, and even socio-economic divisions. As we edge closer to creating expansive digital realities, concerns arise about who owns these spaces, how personal data is used, and what it means for our digital identities. There are also ethical considerations concerning the potential for these platforms to amplify existing societal inequalities. For example, if access to the metaverse becomes a paid privilege, it could further widen the digital divide, excluding those who can't afford it.

Environmental concerns, especially concerning cryptocurrencies and their energy consumption, have become particularly significant. Technologies like Bitcoin have been criticized for their high energy consumption due to proof-of-work algorithms, which require vast amounts of computational power. This has raised concerns about the carbon footprint of such technologies, leading some to question whether the environmental cost is worth the perceived benefits.

Then there is the case of Google Glass. This augmented reality product was promoted as a significant step forward, offering users real-time information overlay on their everyday vision. However, its launch was met with skepticism and even hostility in some quarters. Beyond concerns about fashion or aesthetics, there was a genuine fear about privacy implications. People felt uneasy being filmed or photographed without their knowledge or consent. The term "Glasshole" emerged, portraying wearers as invasive or unaware of social norms. This public backlash led to the device being discontinued for individual consumers.

In a utopian setting, technology serves as the great equalizer. It promises a world where information is freely accessible to all, bridging social divides and creating global communities. Social media platforms would connect distant relatives and friends while virtual reality could simulate experiences, granting everyone a semblance of equality in terms of experiences and knowledge. Advanced medical technology ensures longer, healthier lives while assistive technologies level the playing field for those with disabilities. This is the promise of a tech-driven society, devoid of its complications or constraints, presenting a world united and uplifted by the power of innovation.

In an ideal case scenario, Google Glass stands to profoundly transform everyday experiences. Picture attending a business forum where immediate facial recognition grants attendees with instantaneous data about fellow participants, optimizing networking opportunities. Students, while on educational excursions, could gain enriched insights from instant annotations about historical sites or artifacts. Furthermore, linguistic divides could be effortlessly bridged using the glasses' real-time translation capabilities, enabling seamless global conversations. Given these advantages, who would decline such technology if there were no privacy concerns?

Technology and Society: Finding Common Ground for Progress

Throughout history, society has often met new technological advancements with skepticism and resistance. We've witnessed this with the Luddite movement of the 19th century, the hesitancy towards calculators, and many more. It's a recurring pattern of fear against the unfamiliar, combined with concerns about the implications of new technologies. Now, as we grapple with the advent of AI, the metaverse, and blockchain, similar fears are reemerging, intensified by the sheer complexity and potential of these innovations.

The pushback, often spearheaded by governments and institutional bodies, is rooted in genuine concerns: privacy, surveillance, data misuse, wars, and societal division, to name a few. Yet, this apprehension, while valid, should not deter us from embracing the transformative potential of technology. For it is essential to remember that every technological revolution in history was once met with fear, only to later become normalized and even indispensable to the succeeding generations.

So, let's extrapolate from our past and envision a future where our Gen Alpha and Beta seamlessly integrate with technologies we're only beginning to understand. They'll navigate these platforms with the ease we handle smartphones today, reaping benefits we can scarcely imagine. Their happiness and advancement will be predicated on the technological foundations we're laying now.

Thus, instead of succumbing to fear, we must encourage a dialogue: between the innovators and the skeptics, between the enthusiastic adopters and the cautious holdouts. Governments, policymakers, and society at large should not seek to stifle technology but should instead focus on guiding its trajectory, ensuring it aligns with ethical and societal values. In doing so, we can accelerate technological adoption, ensuring that the promise of a brighter, more connected future becomes a reality for all.

POLITICAL STEERING OF TECHNOLOGICAL EVOLUTION

Governments as Police and Patrons of Progress

Technological evolution is influenced, and at times governed, by the dynamics of political power. Governments, representing collective societal aspirations, can be seen in dual roles: as custodians ensuring order and safety and as promoters of innovation and progress. However, we must not forget that their actions, directions, and intentions often resonate with the motives of policymakers and politicians. The realm of politics is intricate, and many a time, it's less about societal welfare and more about the power play of interests.

Delving into the annals of history, two distinct narratives stand out, showcasing the marriage of politics and technology—the tales of the Enigma machine and the race for nuclear supremacy.

The Enigma machine, an encryption device primarily used by the Germans during World War II, epitomizes the role of technology in warfare and intelligence. It was developed not just as a mere tool but as a strategic weapon, aiming to protect commercial, diplomatic, and, most crucially, military communication. In the hands of the Nazis, it became a formidable instrument, encoding messages that the Allies initially found almost impossible to decrypt. The machine's significance was such that a considerable portion of the war effort by the Allies was dedicated to breaking the Enigma's code. The successful decoding, led by a team including the famed Alan Turing, not only changed the course of the war but also laid the foundations for modern computing. Behind this technological race was the ever-looming shadow of politics and power, where leaders understood that control over information was tantamount to control over the war's outcome.

In parallel, the 20th century witnessed another race, one that was far more explosive—the quest for nuclear technology. Motivated by both the promise of an ultimate weapon and the fear of adversaries gaining the same capability, nations plunged headfirst into nuclear research. This race was not solely about technological prowess but had deep-rooted political implications. Movies like *Oppenheimer* encapsulate the dichotomy of this technology, reflecting both the marvel of human achievement and the haunting shadows it cast over global politics. This race had deep-rooted political implications. The drive for technological supremacy wasn't limited to nuclear power. The mid-20th century's backdrop was marked by the intense rivalry between the two superpowers, both ideologically and militarily. Space exploration became a new frontier where they could showcase their technological, scientific, and political superiority.

In recent times, SpaceX stands as a prime example of how technology, entrepreneurship, and government interests intertwine. Elon Musk's groundbreaking advancements in reusable rocket technology likely would not have progressed so rapidly without aligning with US strategic goals. The conclusion of the Space Shuttle program in 2011 left the US without its own crew transport to the International Space Station, forcing reliance on Russia's Soyuz spacecraft. This dependency underscored NASA's limitations, even with its immense capabilities. Budget constraints and bureaucracy can sometimes slow innovation within the agency, making partnerships with the private sector—like the one they have with SpaceX—essential. This allows for greater flexibility and risk-taking, which are crucial to pushing technological boundaries. Additionally, the US government has a vested interest in maintaining a strong presence in space for reasons of national security and technological leadership.

Through these collaborations, notably with SpaceX, NASA aimed to cultivate a thriving commercial space industry and reestablish America's continuous presence in low Earth orbit. In essence, the confluence of SpaceX's innovations and NASA's strategic goals propelled a new era of space exploration.

In both these narratives, technology wasn't merely an outcome of human progress; it was a tool, a weapon, and often, an instrument maneuvered by the grandmasters of the political arena. As technology continues to shape our future, understanding its past intertwined with politics becomes paramount.

Yet, contrasting this, the world also witnessed cases where the same governmental forces hindered technological growth due to broader concerns. The potential devastation from nuclear technology led to globally coordinated efforts to regulate and monitor its proliferation.

Political Ideologies and Global Tech Diplomacy

The overarching political ideology of a nation or a union heavily dictates how technology is received, integrated, and disseminated. In open democratic settings like France, where individual rights and liberties form the bedrock of governance, policies related to technology might prioritize aspects such as user consent and data privacy. This approach stems from a broader ethos of freedom and personal sovereignty.

However, on the opposite side of the spectrum, we find regimes that prioritize state interests over individual freedoms, like in China. Here, the very same technological tools might be tailored for surveillance, state control, and curbing dissent, aligning with the governing ideology's broader narrative.

Interestingly, the political decisions surrounding technology are not solely a product of ideological stances but also reflect the broader public sentiment. A case in point is the European Union's GDPR. While on the surface, it might appear as a commitment to data privacy in the Digital Age, delving deeper reveals a more complex interplay. GDPR, in many ways, is Europe's answer to the massive data collection dominance by US-based tech giants. It serves both as a shield for individual data rights and a countermeasure to level the playing field in the global data economy. The enactment of such a policy is a dance between reflecting citizens' concerns and catering to broader geopolitical and economic interests.

In our increasingly interconnected world, technological collaborations and conflicts often transcend borders. International regulations, like those governing the internet or space technology, emerge from prolonged negotiations between countries with varied political interests. These negotiations reflect power dynamics, economic dependencies, and future aspirations.

Technologies like AI have become focal points in global geopolitics. Nations recognize the strategic advantage of leading in this field, driving both collaborations and confrontations. This is evident in the race to develop the most powerful language processing AI models, the competition over semiconductor design for AI-specific chips, and the battles over facial recognition technology and its potential for surveillance. Companies like OpenAI (US-based) and Baidu (China-based) are pushing boundaries in these areas, prompting concerns from governments and citizens about potential misuse. This competition isn't just about technological superiority; it reflects a struggle for global influence and control over the digital landscape.

AI-Driven Political System?

As technologies continue to evolve, their interdependence with politics becomes more pronounced. The intertwining of technology and politics can be observed in national strategies like those related to AI or cybersecurity. Governments, recognizing the strategic advantage of certain technologies, might invest heavily in their development. Conversely, technologies that challenge the established order or present perceived threats might face stiff resistance.

Why this resistance? Because these political entities act primarily in their self-interest. Just consider the transformative role social media platforms have played in contemporary politics. Social media has emerged as an influential tool, allowing individuals to challenge governments, voice their concerns, and catalyze change within nations. It provides a platform for collective expression and has been instrumental in movements and protests worldwide.

The role of technology in shaping political landscapes is further evident in how figures like Barack Obama and Donald Trump leveraged the power of social media to rally support and shape narratives during their election campaigns. On the other hand, alleged state-sponsored cyber-attacks, like those attributed to North Korea or Russia, further showcase the intertwined relationship between politics and technology. These are not just random attacks by individual hackers; they are believed to be coordinated actions with political motives to show a certain reality. Additionally, the transformative power of social media isn't limited to politicians: an entire society can challenge their politician or president and effectuate global change through these digital platforms.

Now, projecting into the future, the greatest nightmare for many governments would be the prospect of being replaced by AI. If AI's capabilities grow to a point where it could take on political roles, would an AI-driven political system be more equitable, reducing conflicts and biases? Such a possibility brings with it both hope and apprehension. While the promise of unbiased governance and efficiency is tempting, governments might resist this change, mainly if it's not in their favor. After all, the political world, like any other domain, operates based on vested interests. The true test lies in how these interests align or clash with technological advancements.

The renowned physicist Richard Feynman once said, "The scientific truth may be uncongenial to any particular power, but in the long run it is the only thing that endures and the only thing that gives us any security." This quote sheds light on the complex relationship between scientific progress and political power. By "uncongenial," Feynman means truths that might be inconvenient or disagreeable to those in power. Scientific discoveries often challenge existing paradigms and force re-evaluations of the status quo. Governments, naturally, have a vested interest in maintaining a certain order—one that might be disrupted by these new truths.

However, as Feynman emphasizes, these truths are ultimately enduring. They hold validity regardless of political agendas or short-term anxieties. The "security" he mentions comes from understanding the real nature of the world, a foundation for effective decision-making and long-term progress. In the context of our discussion about technology and politics, this is a reminder for us that even transformative technologies might face resistance from powerful entities who fear a loss of control.

ECONOMIC LEVERS CONTROLLING TECHNOLOGICAL GROWTH
Technology and Economic Advantage of Countries

In technological terms, "democratized technology" refers to systems and tools designed to be open and accessible, allowing widespread participation from diverse groups regardless of economic or social status. This approach encourages shared innovation and collective problem-solving, often facilitated by open-source models or affordable technology platforms. Conversely, "centralized technology" involves systems and resources being controlled and maintained by a select few organizations or entities, leading to concentrated power and influence.

An interesting case here is OpenAI, which can be seen from both perspectives. On one hand, it democratizes technology by providing access to advanced AI tools like the GPT models via APIs, enabling developers globally to build a myriad of applications. On the other hand, the development and control of these models are centralized, with OpenAI managing access, updates, and pricing, which exemplifies the centralized technology model.

The drive towards more democratized technology holds profound economic implications. Centralization often leads to monopolistic behavior, potentially limiting innovation and leading to economic disparities. Conversely, democratization can foster a more competitive landscape, promote grassroots innovation, and potentially lead to a more equitable distribution of economic benefits.

However, it's also essential to understand that while democratization brings many advantages, it also poses challenges. In the broader context, the democratization of technology could be a powerful force in leveling the economic playing field, ensuring that the benefits of innovation are not confined to a select few but are accessible to a broader population. The challenge lies in harnessing this trend while mitigating potential pitfalls.

The race to harness technology for economic advantage has become a central theme for countries in the 21st century. Nations worldwide are increasingly recognizing the transformative power of technology, especially in sectors such as infrastructure, urban planning, and services. A key example of this movement is the concept of a "smart city," where integrated tech solutions aim to enhance residents' quality of life while promoting sustainable growth.

Dubai stands as a testament to this vision. Over the years, it has pioneered the transformation into a smart city, incorporating technology into various facets of its urban ecosystem. From intelligent traffic systems to digital public services, the city has leveraged innovations to streamline operations and enhance citizen experiences. This tech-centric approach has not only elevated Dubai's global standing but also markedly improved its residents' lives.

This advancement isn't just about enhancing urban aesthetics or conveniences; it's deeply intertwined with economic prosperity. As cities become smarter, they can operate more efficiently, reduce wastage, ensure quicker service delivery, and create a favorable environment for businesses. Such an environment, in turn, attracts more investments, fosters innovation, and drives economic growth. With the vast amounts of data generated in these cities, digital infrastructure can optimize resources and personalize services, leading to increased customer happiness and loyalty.

While the "smart city" concept offers undeniable advantages—from efficiency to economic growth—a crucial question emerges: will these cities truly serve the well-being of their residents, or will they be optimized solely for consumption and profit? This potential pitfall highlights the need for a new urban paradigm.

Enter the "cognitive city." These cities leverage technologies such as AI, robotics, internet of things (IoT), and blockchain to become intelligent, adaptable ecosystems that learn and evolve to improve citizens' lives. Imagine a city that anticipates your needs, streamlines daily routines, and fosters a thriving, healthy community. This is where technology transcends mere convenience and empowers individuals to "live well."

These cities are not just technologically advanced but are also capable of learning from data, evolving to changing circumstances, and proactively delivering services to enhance the well-being and livability of their inhabitants—truly embodying the idea of "dying alive" in an environment that continuously learns and adapts to ensure that its inhabitants can thrive.

Saudi Arabia, through its giga projects like Neom, serves as a global testbed for this innovative concept. These projects aim to integrate cognitive technologies across various sectors including real estate and construction, retail, financial services, public safety, healthcare, and education. This vast implementation highlights the transformative potential, as Joseph Bradley, CEO of technology and digital at Neom, tells WIRED: "While smart cities only use 1% of the data generated by residents, a cognitive city will leverage more than 90%."[1] This leap in data usage underscores the impact cognitive cities can have on the overall human experience, particularly in streamlining access to vital services like education and digital healthcare.

While European nations were among the early adopters of such technological advancements, the momentum has now visibly shifted. Middle Eastern countries, notably the UAE and KSA, have surged to the forefront. Their leadership recognizes the immense value and potential of integrating technology into their economic fabric. The UAE, for instance, has set its sights on becoming a global hub for AI by 2031, projecting that AI will contribute almost 14% to the UAE's GDP by that year.

China, with its vast consumer and industrial application markets, serves as another compelling example of rapid AI development. The nation ranks second on the Global AI Innovation Index for three consecutive years, and its core AI industry is valued at over $68 billion. The rapid development of AI is projected to create new economic growth areas, accelerating the expansion of digital industries and facilitating the intelligent upgrade of traditional sectors such as education, medicine, and transportation.

It's important to note that this accelerated tech adoption is influenced by the governance structures in these countries. In contrast to more democratic countries where public debate and potential opposition might slow down implementation, these nations can enact technological change at a faster pace. This raises complex questions about the trade-offs between rapid innovation and the role of public input in shaping technological development. For example, China's ambitious social credit system leverages AI and big data to monitor and influence citizen behavior. While this system boasts efficiency and benefits to well-being and security, concerns about privacy and government control remain prevalent.

The Economic Boon and Bane of Tech Developments

The double-edged sword of technological progression carries with it both promises and challenges. The ripples of innovation are felt not just in isolated sectors, but throughout the very fabric of global economies. While the narrative often shifts towards the potential dangers posed by tech developments, especially regarding job displacement, a closer inspection reveals a more nuanced picture.

At a fundamental level, every technological disruption has led to societal reconfigurations. The introduction of the automobile, for instance, might have made horse-drawn carriages obsolete, but it birthed an entire industry, from manufacturing to servicing, that employed millions. The same principle applies to today's advancements.

Indeed, while automation and AI may reduce demand for certain traditional roles, they simultaneously give rise to a plethora of novel professions and sectors. Consider the gig economy: platforms like Uber, Airbnb, and TaskRabbit have democratized employment, offering flexible work schedules and breaking the standards of a conventional 9-to-5 job. These platforms have not only created employment for millions but have also provided consumers with more efficient, often cheaper, services.

Similarly, the Digital Age has catapulted the rise of content creators—YouTubers, bloggers, influencers, and podcasters, to name a few. These professions, largely unheard of two decades ago, now form a thriving ecosystem, providing livelihoods to many while also influencing global consumer patterns.

Moreover, technology has also facilitated the rise of remote work and digital nomadism. With the advent of reliable internet and collaborative tools, one can work from virtually anywhere, leading to a decentralization of job markets. This has created opportunities for talent in regions previously inaccessible, bridging economic disparities to some extent.

However, these changes are not without their challenges. The gig economy, while offering flexibility, often lacks the job security and benefits associated with traditional employment. Similarly, the rapid pace of technological advancements means that continuous learning and skill adaptation become imperative to remain relevant.

In essence, technology's economic impact is multifaceted. While certain sectors may contract, many others expand, and entirely new ones are birthed. The key lies in adaptability. Societies, educational institutions, and governments must anticipate these shifts and equip their populations with the skills and mindsets needed for this ever-evolving landscape. However, individuals also hold responsibility for how they respond to these technological shifts. Building awareness about the benefits and potential risks, along with the confidence to play a role in shaping technology's adoption, empowers us all to be active participants in the future. Chapters 2 and 4 delve deeper into this, exploring both individual actions and systemic solutions. Specifically, Chapter 4 highlights the importance of becoming informed about algorithms, managing our digital footprint, and understanding how our online behaviors influence systems that impact our lives to better respond to technological changes. Only with proactive measures can we ensure that the scales of technological development tilt more towards boon than bane.

Technology for Global Progress: A Call for International Cooperation

Technology, in its essence, is neither the problem nor the panacea; it's the application and management of it that determines its societal impact. As we tread deeper into the Digital Age, understanding the dual nature of technology becomes crucial—it simultaneously presents unparalleled opportunities and equally imposing challenges.

The question isn't simply about jobs being eliminated. It's also about how jobs will transform. Historically, every major technological shift, from the Industrial Revolution to the Information Age, has led to the displacement of certain roles. However, they have concurrently paved the way for new roles we couldn't have imagined. Our economy, inherently dynamic, constantly undergoes this cycle of job destruction and creation.

Yet, as rightly pointed out, the modern labor landscape has evolved. The "new era of labor" is characterized by flexibility, dynamism, and, unfortunately, a degree of insecurity. Instead of conventional full-time roles with comprehensive benefits, we see a surge in gig roles, freelance work, and contractual engagements. However, with this change comes an unprecedented level of autonomy and entrepreneurial spirit. This transformation is not inherently negative, but it demands adaptability and resilience from the workforce.

Furthermore, the undeniable link between technological advancements and economic growth cannot be overlooked. As industries innovate and processes become more efficient, there is potential for increased profitability, national GDP growth, and even a global economic boost. However, this potential relies on ensuring that the benefits of innovation reach everyone in society, not just a select few.

Governments indeed have a pivotal role to play. The concerns voiced—about the security of these new-age jobs and the overarching economic growth—need to be at the forefront of policymaking. It's high time national strategies be realigned, prioritizing education, skill development, and social security nets. Preparing the workforce for this dynamic environment and ensuring their well-being should be non-negotiable.

Moreover, in this age of interconnectedness, isolationist policies won't suffice. Economic diplomacy, fostering international collaborations, and shared technological endeavors will be instrumental. These collaborative ventures can ensure a more balanced technological and economic landscape where shared growth and prosperity are tangible goals.

In conclusion, as we navigate this tumultuous yet exhilarating technological era, the focus should remain on harnessing its potential for the collective good. Only with shared responsibility, foresight, and collaboration can we ensure that technology remains a beacon of progress for all of humanity.

Navigating the Intersections of Society, Politics, and Economy

To comprehensively understand the challenges faced in the integration of technology within the three dimensions of society, politics, and the economy, it's imperative to highlight some fundamental roadblocks. There exists a palpable lack of consensus within governments and other significant stakeholders on the approach towards the adoption of new technologies, particularly AI. This disharmony often stems from short-term thinking, where the emphasis is placed on immediate resolutions rather than forward-looking investments that would set the foundation for a technologically advanced future.

A critical challenge many governments seem to face also arises from the difficulty, or perhaps reluctance, to measure the potential return on investment (ROI) for technological investments like AI. It's further worsened by an environment of political polarization, which hinders cooperation across party lines. This divisive atmosphere does more than just obstruct technological progress; it challenges the very foundation of collective decision-making. Lastly, budgetary constraints remain a persistent concern. In a world where technological advancement often requires significant spending, the difficulty in securing necessary funding can delay or slow the pace of innovation.

Analyzing these dynamics within the framework of society, politics, and the economy deepens our understanding. It brings to the fore the necessity of achieving harmony among these pillars, underlining that the role of technology extends beyond mere invention to its judicious integration within our societal constructs. In concluding, the discourse leaves us with key questions:

- Can we find a delicate balance that interweaves the often-conflicting demands of society, politics, and the economy in the age of rapid technological evolution?
- What proactive steps can individuals and society at large undertake to ensure the responsible and beneficial integration of technology into the fabric of our society? Moreover, what systemic solutions should politicians and policymakers implement to harmonize these digital domains?
- As we ponder the transformative potential of technology, how can ethical considerations remain at the core of our endeavors, guiding the trajectory of our shared digital future?

Navigating these realms necessitates a holistic perspective, appreciating the interconnectedness of society, politics, and the economy. Addressing the multifaceted challenges and harnessing the opportunities will demand a synergized approach that transcends traditional boundaries. As we stand at the crossroads of a digital revolution, the choices we make now will delineate the course of human progress for generations to come.

Moving forward, the upcoming chapter expands on these ideas, delving into the actions we can take to turn the digital revolution into an era of unprecedented progress. This next chapter will explore how integrating technology into our lives and workspaces should empower us, not diminish us. It's about laying the groundwork for generations to come, ensuring they inherit the tools and systems to become the "Die Alive" generations of the future.

CHAPTER 1 TAKEAWAYS

Technology and society are inseparable, with societal values and fears shaping how technologies are accepted or resisted.

Politics and technology are intertwined, sometimes to government leaders' approval and other times not. Governments sometimes push for particular innovations. They might partner with private entities to fuel particular progress. However, governments might resist certain technologies that disrupt their power structures.

Technology transforms economies. Nations vying for leadership in AI or smart infrastructure, like Dubai, understand the economic benefits. While automation has risks, history shows that technological shifts create new industries and jobs like the gig economy. The challenge is ensuring these benefits are widely shared.

Collaboration is crucial for successfully navigating technology's complexities. Governments, policymakers, and societies must find common ground and foster open dialogue. We need to move past fear and ensure ethical, beneficial outcomes.

UNIFYING DIGITAL REALMS: INDIVIDUAL ACTIONS, SYSTEMIC SOLUTIONS

There's a strong tendency to think that what we have today is the ultimate, that we basically created the world in its current form 20 to 50 years ago, and it will always be this way ... The reality is that the world changes very rapidly.

—Ray Kurzweil, computer scientist, author, inventor, and futurist

Whenever I encounter the oft-repeated question of whether AI and machines will replace our jobs, I'm prompted to smile. It's a real concern for many, but it feels like an old story that doesn't get questioned enough. I find myself wondering, "Do people truly expect the landscape of work to remain unchanged for decades?" It's a bit like expecting a city skyline will never change over the years. The truth is, our economy is a living, breathing thing, always in circular motion, perpetually evolving—just as the boundless galaxy never stops expanding.

The fear of a jobless future is misplaced and unrealistic. We are on the brink of an era filled with unprecedented types of work, novel business ventures, and opportunities yet to be imagined. Instead of fearing obsolescence, let's embrace the excitement of what's to come. Prepare not for an end but for a beginning—the emergence of new vocations as technology advances, beckoning us to contribute, create, and help the world navigate towards these promising systemic solutions.

The question, "What can WE, as individuals, do?" resonates with a potency that demands our attention. It's about using technology judiciously, remaining lifelong learners, and embodying the resilience and adaptability mirrored in our own devices. It calls for us to focus on and champion the indispensable qualities that make us human—our care for others, our empathy, our curiosity, and our ability to invent—and allow technology to serve us, alleviating the burden of tasks and enabling a focus beyond the capitalist drive for production. This is not about tech innovations working to merely satisfy the bottom line or entertain us while waiting in line or commuting to work; it's about enriching the fabric of society.

In contrast, there's the question, "What can THEY, as systems, do?" Dialogue around this question began in Chapter 1, where we considered the influence of governments, society, and policymakers. There is untapped potential in collective, strategic action that can profoundly improve both our digital existence and our tangible reality. Envision, as an initial step, the establishment of a model city—a testbed for innovative ideas that could demonstrate value and impact, setting a precedent for global emulation.

Our choices today are the architects of tomorrow. Infused with insights from Brynjolfsson and McAfee's *The Second Machine Age*, this chapter endeavors not only to navigate the currents of digital transformation but also to distill from their wisdom actionable recommendations. Together, we will chart a course that empowers both individuals and systems to harness the full potential of our technological dawn, ensuring that its benefits reach every corner of society.

EDUCATION AS A CORNERSTONE

Education has always been a battlefield for progress, with visionaries throughout history pushing against the status quo. Socrates, the ancient Greek philosopher, famously critiqued his society's educational methods, emphasizing the need for critical thinking over rote memorization. His dissent is an early echo of a debate that has continued through the ages, with each era bringing its own champions for change.

The Enlightenment further revolutionized education, with thinkers such as Rousseau and Kant advocating for a more rational and empirical approach to learning. They sought to enlighten minds, promoting reason and science as the cornerstones of knowledge.

Fast forward to the early 20th century, where the progressive education movement, led by figures like John Dewey, championed student-centered learning. They believed in the power of hands-on experience, creativity, and problem-solving within education to prepare children for the complexities of life.

Movements for social justice have also played a significant role in reshaping education. The civil rights movement fought tirelessly for the desegregation of schools in America while the feminist movement worked to dismantle gender biases in classrooms, ensuring equal opportunities for all genders.

In more recent times, the forces of globalization have spurred an emphasis on cross-cultural understanding and international education. The Digital Age has brought the global community closer, making it more important than ever to understand diverse perspectives and navigate a world without borders.

Now, as we stand at the frontier of the second machine age, the call for educational reform is loud and clear. It's about expanding our educational buffet to include a vast array of subjects and learning methods tailored to the interests and abilities of each student. No longer is it enough to follow a one-size-fits-all approach; education must become as diverse and dynamic as the world it prepares us for.

Technology integration into education is more than a mere upgrade; it's a fundamental shift in how we teach and learn. By leveraging tech tools, we can bring complex subjects to life, making them accessible and engaging for every learner. Learning and repeating what has been taught does not evolve us as human beings; instead, engaging our brains and neurons through diverse inputs and encouraging innovative outputs is what enables us to innovate.

Imagine a K to 12 educational system where students are evaluated not just on their ability to memorize formulas but on their capacity for critical thinking. For example, while traditional systems have insisted on rote learning of theoretical formulas, alongside practical labs, the accessibility of AI and public information online now obviates the need for memorizing these formulas. Instead, we can use virtual reality and extended reality to help students understand complex concepts and then challenge them in exams or assignments with open-ended research and development questions that demand innovative solutions. This approach could nurture young researcher-like students, fostering a generation that leverages their untapped cerebral potential from a young age. Although this may draw criticism, it's crucial to recognize that we often underestimate the capabilities of our own brains, especially in young students.

Thus, our investment in education must be strategic, focusing on fostering creativity, innovation, and a lifelong appetite for learning. By doing so, we can create a synergy between human potential and technological advancement, ensuring they amplify each other, propelling society forward. This isn't just about preparing students for the job market; it's about equipping them to navigate and shape the future, continuing the legacy of educational reformers throughout history.

As we draw from the past and look to the future, a question arises: what if we dared to challenge the very foundations of our educational systems? What if we no longer accepted the rigid structures of the past and instead embraced a more fluid, personalized form of learning? Envision an educational model that ignites a child's passion for astronomy at the tender age of ten or nurtures another's fascination with philosophy from the earliest curiosity. By deeply assessing each student's aptitudes and interests through advanced technological tools, we can craft a learning path that resonates with their inherent strengths and passions.

This vision harnesses the power of technology—such as AI-driven analytics, machine learning, and cognitive assessment tools—to dynamically evaluate and adapt to each student's unique learning needs and preferences. These technologies can analyze a vast array of data points from student interactions within learning platforms, enabling educators to tailor educational content that not only aligns with individual aptitudes but also stimulates engagement and enthusiasm. Imagine adaptive learning systems that evolve in real-time, presenting challenges that are perfectly pitched to each student's level of understanding and interest. Such a system wouldn't just teach; it would inspire, encourage exploration, and foster a lifelong love of learning by making education a deeply personal and empowering experience.

This approach shifts the focus from a one-size-fits-all curriculum to a truly individualized educational journey, ensuring that every student not only learns but thrives by engaging deeply with subjects that they are passionate about. By integrating these technologies into our educational frameworks, we open a world of possibilities where every child's educational experience is as unique as they are, paving the way for a future where education is not just about information acquisition but about nurturing innovators, thinkers, and leaders.

This call to action is not just about choice—it's about relevance and engagement. It's about recognizing that a student who is impassioned by a subject will pursue it with a vigor that can't be instilled through compulsion. When education aligns with a student's innate interests, it ceases to be a chore and becomes a joy, a quest for knowledge that is self-driven and self-sustaining. It's evident that our educational institutions must pivot from their age-old trajectories and evolve. They need to become arenas of discovery and innovation, where technology aids in tailoring education to fit the individual, not the mass.

Through assessment platforms that leverage AI to identify a student's unique learning styles and strengths, adaptive learning programs could then craft individualized lesson plans, adjusting content and pace to ensure optimal understanding. Virtual and augmented reality experiences could make historical events come alive or provide hands-on simulations of scientific concepts. With the power of technology, we can help students not just find their places in the world but carve out new ones—places where their knowledge and talents meet the needs of a society in constant motion through the second machine age.

While the exact form of these technologies continues to evolve rapidly, in later chapters (specifically Chapter 7), we'll explore specific examples and discuss how they can transform the educational landscape.

In this reimagined educational landscape, we're not just imparting knowledge; we're inspiring a new generation of thinkers, creators, and innovators. We're not preparing students for a predetermined career; we're equipping them with the skills to craft their own and build new careers. Students trapped in outdated educational models may feel "born dead," i.e., limited by systems that stifle their potential. Yet, by embracing the power of technology within our classrooms, we prepare future generations to the concept of "dying alive." No longer constrained by systems that limit their potential, our students become creators and pioneers, empowered to extend the reach of human knowledge. They discover the thrill of exploration and the deep satisfaction of innovation. It's a bold step—and a necessary one—to seize the transformative potential of the digital era. This is how we ensure education remains not just a societal cornerstone, but a dynamic and evolving launchpad for human progress.

INVESTING IN SCIENCE AND R&D

In the symphony of progress that characterizes our second machine age, science and research and development (R&D) conduct the movement. The innovations we witness today, the leaps in artificial intelligence, biotechnology, and sustainable energy, all stem from the seeds of research sown yesterday. Yet, despite the clear link between R&D and advancement, our current systems often fail to adequately fuel the very engines that drive progress.

Real numbers reflect this disparity. For instance, despite the clear need for continued innovation, the percentage of GDP that many countries allocate to R&D has remained relatively flat or even declined in recent years. The UNESCO Science Report from 2021 stated, the "race against time for smarter development" highlights a concerning trend: roughly 80% of countries still invest less than 1% of GDP in R&D.[1] In some cases, the researcher population has risen faster than related expenditure, leaving less funding available to each researcher. This signifies a need for urgent change. We must prioritize investment in research and development if we hope to create a more sustainable, equitable, and innovative future.

Why is it that the lifelines of scientific endeavor—funding and support—are often so constricted? Consider the plight of scientists whose groundbreaking ideas languish due to a lack of resources or the potential technologies that remain on the drawing board, unrealized due to fiscal shortsightedness. Brynjolfsson and McAfee remind us that investment in R&D is a critical driver for economic growth and societal well-being, yet the reality often falls short of the ideal.

The question then arises: what if our investment in science and R&D matched the magnitude of our reliance on the fruits of these fields? Imagine the possibilities if the funding and encouragement of scientists were as robust as the public's use of technology. Current systems seem to awaken to the necessity of R&D only when a dire need surfaces— when a pandemic demands a vaccine or when an environmental crisis calls for clean energy solutions. It is a reactive stance, born of immediate need rather than a proactive, visionary approach.

Why do we typically only invest in innovation when there's an urgent need, instead of giving it the steady support it requires? Consider the arduous journey of medical research: for decades, brilliant minds have been in pursuit of cures for cancers, yet the pace can feel glacial, the breakthroughs incremental. It prompts a pressing question: what if our support for scientific research was as persistent and enduring as the maladies we seek to overcome?

Imagine a world where funding for science isn't an afterthought but a foresight. Imagine the bounds of medicine leaping forward, where the elusive cure for Alzheimer's or the final blow to cancer could be just within our reach, no longer hindered by the droughts of funding. The aforementioned UNESCO Science Report reflects a sobering reality— the R&D expenditure, while essential, often fails to meet the urgency of these quests.[2]

Ponder for a moment the realms of physics, where the mysteries of bosons and quarks suggest possibilities that border science fiction. What if R&D investment allowed us to unravel these mysteries? Could we one day speak not just of traveling at the speed of light as a theoretical marvel but as a tangible goal? The implications are staggering—a paradigm shift in how we perceive travel, communication, and our very concept of distance. This isn't just about scientific advancement; it's about transcending our current limitations and transforming our understanding of the universe. In a world where such profound knowledge is within our grasp, we embody the ethos of being "born dead," awakening to the infinite possibilities of our existence, and striving to "die alive"— to having fully explored and expanded the frontiers of human potential.

On the other hand, there's a noticeable disparity between industries, particularly evident when comparing the entertainment sector to scientific fields. For instance, the earnings of a singer can surpass those of a scientist, raising critical questions about our societal priorities and values. Why does entertainment often command a higher monetary value than the contributions of those driving technological and medical innovations?

This disparity becomes even more intriguing when considering the future impact of AI and robotics. Automation and AI are increasingly capable of replicating aspects of creativity and entertainment, potentially reducing the need for human involvement in these areas. This shift could lead to a renewed interest in professions that require intensive human intellect, such as scientific research, which AI and robots cannot easily replicate.

Acknowledging this, there is a need to reassess how we value and financially reward scientific work. Aligning the remuneration of scientists with the significant impact of their contributions could encourage more sustained and ambitious investment in R&D. A society that values and invests in scientific minds is one that is preparing for a future where innovation is not left to chance but is a result of deliberate planning and support.

By robustly investing in R&D, we not only address the current financial imbalance but also lay the foundation for a future where progress in fields like quantum physics or medical research is fostered and adequately supported. This approach would redefine the future, where limitations are set not by resources but by our collective imagination and where the architects of progress are recognized for their indispensable role in advancing society.

We need to advocate for a future where our investment in science and R&D echoes the grandeur of our aspirations. It's a call to break free from the reactive shackles of "too little, too late" and step into a world where scientific discovery is limited only by our imagination. It's a call for an era where the next monumental discovery in quantum physics or the next medical miracle is a product of deliberate intent, not fortunate happenstance. In this second machine age, let's not just dream of such advancements; let's fund, support, and realize them.

EVOLVING THE LABOR MARKET

In the landscape shaped by the second machine age, the labor market is poised for significant transformation. The rise of intelligent machines often stirs fears of job displacement, but as highlighted in *The Second Machine Age* by Brynjolfsson and McAfee, the future is more about augmentation and diversity in employment than obsolescence. This is a future where human work is complemented and enhanced by technology, not replaced by it.

The evolution of the labor market calls for a workforce that is not only technologically adept but also proficient in areas where human empathy and judgment are irreplaceable. This notion extends beyond the mere acquisition of new skills; it's about a fundamental change in the employment landscape, where diversification of careers is not just possible but encouraged. In this dynamic employment landscape shaped by the second machine age, the concept of holding a single job for life is becoming increasingly archaic. The advent of intelligent machines, often perceived as a threat to job security, is actually facilitating a shift towards a more diverse and enriched labor market.

Today, we observe an emerging trend, especially among Generation Y, where individuals aspire to pursue multiple vocations concurrently. This multifaceted career approach, however, often clashes with traditional employment models and mindsets. Many in this generation, and the following Generation Z, are seeking to blend their professions with their passions and hobbies. Yet, there is a gap between this aspiration and the opportunities available, stemming from a rigid corporate culture that has yet to adapt to this paradigm shift. This evolution resonates personally with my aspirations and the aspirations of many in my generation.

For instance, if I were to fully embrace this new paradigm, my professional life would be a tapestry of varied roles and interests. I envision myself as a strategy consultant, an author, and a public speaker, intertwining these roles with the entrepreneurial drive of a startup founder and the community spirit of an association founder. Beyond these, I would realize my childhood dream, delving into a doctorate in engineering, specifically targeting scientific research related to space exploration. This blend of professions, once an unconventional dream, can now become a feasible reality.

However, achieving this dream requires a paradigm shift in the workplace. Employers need to recognize and support the pursuit of multiple careers. This support isn't just about allowing employees to take on other roles; it's about acknowledging that fulfilling diverse professional interests can lead to more engaged, satisfied, and productive employees. As long as primary job objectives are met, secondary or parallel careers should not only be permitted but encouraged by employers.

This trend towards career diversity is already visible on platforms like LinkedIn, where individuals proudly display multiple job titles and roles. It's a clear indication that the workforce is ready and willing to embrace a variety of responsibilities and interests. The narrative is changing: having multiple jobs is no longer seen as a sign of indecision or lack of commitment but as a testament to an individual's multifaceted skills and their adaptability in a dynamic job market.

The potential displacement of jobs by AI and automation is not a dead-end but an opportunity for career evolution. As some roles become automated, new ones will emerge, and individuals will have the opportunity to contribute to multiple fields, diversifying their skills and income sources. The future of work is not about limiting oneself to a single job; it's about expanding horizons and embracing the multitude of opportunities that the second machine age offers.

In this new era, the concept of a singular career path is giving way to a more dynamic, fluid approach to professional development. It's an approach that not only accommodates but celebrates the diverse interests and capabilities of each individual. As technology continues to transform the labor market, our approach to careers and employment must evolve in tandem, ensuring a future where the workforce is as diverse, versatile, and vibrant as the technology that propels it. This philosophy encourages us to explore fully, engage deeply, and remain vibrant and "alive" in our professional pursuits, leveraging every opportunity to grow and excel in a technology-driven world.

TIME FOR BOTS HIRING?

In a fascinating turn of events, reflecting the deepening integration of AI in the corporate world, there have been actual instances where AI systems have assumed CEO-like roles. For example, China-based NetDragon Websoft appointed an AI program named Tang Yu as its CEO in August. Tasked with supporting decision-making in the company's daily operations, this "AI-powered virtual humanoid robot" has notably outperformed Hong Kong's Hang Seng Index in the six months since its appointment. This development might sound like a scenario straight out of science fiction, but it's a burgeoning reality.

Does this represent a threat to traditional leadership roles? Interestingly, not at all. Consider the core responsibilities of a CEO or a high-level executive. It's not about executing routine tasks, designing products, or managing day-to-day operations. At its essence, leadership is about strategic decision-making, overseeing business trajectories, allocating budgets, and, importantly, making fair and unbiased decisions. This is where AI can play a transformative role.

An AI, devoid of human biases, is not swayed by politics, personal preferences, or hidden agendas. Its decisions are based on data, patterns, and logical predictions. In this context, AI's role in leadership can be seen as an opportunity to enhance fairness and ethical decision-making in business. It's about complementing human leadership with AI's capacity for impartial analysis and decision-making.

However, this doesn't diminish the value of human qualities in leadership—empathy, creativity, and intuition remain irreplaceable. Instead, envision a future where AI and human leaders work in tandem, each playing to their strengths. AI can handle data-driven decisions and impartial allocations while human executives focus on vision, innovation, and the human aspects of business leadership.

This synergy could usher in a new era of corporate governance, one characterized by a blend of human insight and AI efficiency. It's a future where leadership is not just about making decisions but making them wisely and fairly, with a blend of human empathy and AI-driven impartiality. As we embrace this new age of technological integration, the possibilities for reshaping the traditional paradigms of work and leadership are not just promising but limitless.

TOOLS AND INFRASTRUCTURES

In our journey through the second machine age, the importance of sophisticated matchmaking platforms in reshaping the labor market cannot be overstated. While LinkedIn has been a frontrunner in this domain, the landscape is ripe for a multitude of diverse platforms, each tailored to meet specific needs and niches in the job market. The call to action for private entities is clear: there is immense potential in developing platforms that not only connect job seekers with opportunities but also bridge gaps between skills and market needs.

Envision a future where digital platforms extend beyond the realms of LinkedIn, offering a variety of services from career pathing to mentorship connections. These platforms could leverage advanced algorithms and robust infrastructures to provide accurate and efficient matches. They could identify emerging job trends, align skills with market demands, and offer personalized development pathways to users.

The role of enhanced infrastructures in these platforms is critical. They should be designed to handle vast amounts of data securely and efficiently, ensuring user trust and system reliability. This involves employing state-of-the-art technologies in data management and analysis, ensuring that the platform not only connects people to jobs but also provides insights into career growth and industry trends.

These platforms could revolutionize how we view and engage with the labor market. By offering more than just job listings, they could become holistic career development hubs. They could cater to diverse sectors, from tech to creative industries, providing a space where both traditional and unconventional career paths are explored and nurtured.

Moreover, these platforms could democratize access to opportunities. By breaking geographical barriers and providing equal visibility to all talent, they could ensure that the best matches are made based on skills and compatibility, not just proximity or familiarity.

As we forge ahead in the second machine age, the development of such platforms is imperative. They hold the key to a more dynamic, inclusive, and efficient workforce. The future of work hinges on our ability to effectively match the right talent with the right opportunities, and in this endeavor, the next generation of matchmaking platforms will play a pivotal role.

BUILDING BLOCKS FOR TECHNOLOGICAL ENABLEMENT
Fostering Startups and Innovation

Startups are the lifeblood of innovation in the technology sector. They embody the spirit of the second machine age—agile, disruptive, and forward-thinking. Encouraging these ventures means more than just providing financial backing; it requires a nurturing ecosystem. This ecosystem consists of a supportive policy environment, access to talent, and a culture that celebrates risk-taking and tolerates failure. Brynjolfsson and McAfee's work suggests that such an environment could lead to a flourishing landscape of technological innovation, one that could yield solutions to some of our most pressing challenges.

Building Infrastructure and Incentives

The digital divide can be bridged with the right infrastructure in place. This encompasses not just the physical components like broadband and sensors but also the soft infrastructure of data standards and privacy protections. Incentives play a critical role here, encouraging investments in areas that may not offer immediate financial returns but are critical for long-term sustainability. Tax incentives, subsidies, and grants can all be used to stimulate growth in strategic technological sectors.

Adaptive Tools and Taxation

In the hands of a well-informed policy framework, tools and AI can become powerful allies in societal development. Adaptive tools that leverage AI's capabilities can transform sectors like healthcare, education, and transportation. Tax policies that support R&D in these areas can accelerate innovation. Drawing on the philosophy of *The Second Machine Age*, these fiscal strategies must be designed not just with the current technological landscape in mind but also for the emerging and future trends.

Policy, Governance, and Public Engagement

Finally, robust policy and governance structures must underpin all technological advancement. Transparent, participatory governance that includes public engagement ensures that the direction of technology aligns with societal values and needs. As Brynjolfsson and McAfee articulate, awareness and dialogue are key in guiding the ethical development and deployment of technology. It's about creating a shared vision where technology serves the common good, paving the way for a future where progress is measured not just by the gadgets that we invent but by the lives that we enhance.

As we conclude Chapter 2, we recognize the transformative potential technology holds for individual and systemic change, from reshaping our labor markets to revolutionizing our educational paradigms. These discussions have set a firm groundwork, illustrating how technological advances can be leveraged to enrich and diversify our professional and personal lives. Moving into Chapter 3, "Unveiling the 'True' Value," we shift our focus towards rethinking traditional measures of progress and success, advocating for new metrics that better reflect the profound influence of technology on societal well-being and happiness.

CHAPTER 2 TAKEAWAYS

The second machine age demands a revolution in how we approach education, work, and the role of technology in society. Education must ditch one-size-fits-all models and embrace personalized learning. We need to ignite students' passions, tailoring education to individual strengths while fostering critical thinking, creativity, and a lifelong love of learning. Technology should be integrated to make subjects engaging and accessible.

Science and R&D are engines of innovation, but funding is often inadequate. We need long-term, proactive investment in science, matching our reliance on its outcomes. This will unlock cures, sustainable solutions, and a future where progress isn't hindered by lack of resources.

The workplace is transforming. The focus must be on adaptability and skills where humans excel: empathy, judgment, and creativity. People should be encouraged to pursue multiple careers at once, with employers embracing this fluidity. AI can augment leadership by providing unbiased decision-making support.

New tools like advanced digital platforms can revolutionize job matching, offering career guidance and mentorship to create a more dynamic workforce.

Beyond this we must nurture startups, build reliable infrastructure, use AI ethically with public input, and create policies aligned with both present needs and the unpredictable future. Only then can technology truly serve society and improve lives.

CHAPTER 3

UNVEILING THE "TRUE" VALUE

The gross national product does not allow for the health of our children, the quality of their education, or the joy of their play. It does not include the beauty of our poetry or the strength of our marriages; the intelligence of our public debate or the integrity of our public officials ... It measures neither our wit nor our courage; neither our wisdom nor our learning; neither our compassion nor our devotion to our country; it measures everything, in short, except that which makes life worthwhile.

—Robert F. Kennedy

B ack when I was in school, there was a question that always popped up: "What do you think the world will look like in the next two or three decades?" It was a simple yet thought-provoking question, inviting a surge of imaginative ideas. If you pause and think, you've likely been asked a version of this same question at some point in your life. After all, to repeat—it's a simple yet thought-provoking question, inviting a surge of imaginative ideas.

Most of my friends, including me, came up with incredible, futuristic visions. Floating cars, teleportation, and getting food just by hitting a button.

It's funny, when asked to envision the future, most people extrapolate from the present, adding a touch of the fantastical. For example, in my childhood world, because roads were a limitation, in the future cars would simply float. Teleportation was the solution to escape boring classes or difficult situations. And invisibility? Well, that was just the ultimate tool for uncovering hidden knowledge. Interestingly, even now, some of the most outlandish tech ideas begin with questioning the seemingly fundamental constraints of our world.

Innovations often unfold beneath the surface; they're built on countless smaller steps. We might imagine technology advancing in explosive bursts, but the reality is often a gradual climb. This aligns with the principle of exponential growth—progress may seem slow initially, then rapidly accelerates as the foundation is laid. Research takes time, and sometimes those groundbreaking announcements take decades to fully materialize in our daily lives.

Now, 20 years later, I can't help but smile. Things didn't turn out quite how our young minds imagined. We dreamed so big back then, but the reality of technological progress is more complex. Often, the most significant changes aren't immediately obvious. Just think—moving from the first telephone to free global video calls on WhatsApp feels like a massive leap. Yet, currently the metaverse—where you see and interact with your folks in 3D right in your room—still seems like science fiction, a glimpse into a future just beyond our reach. But could it be closer than we think?

The truth is, technological progress often follows a pattern of hidden potential. Just look at the leap from the first telephones to free global video calls—a revolution fueled by countless smaller advancements. The metaverse may seem like a giant leap, but it's likely built upon a foundation of incremental innovations happening right now.

Today, I confidently hold a belief, so strong and bold that it might seem audacious to some, in the power of turning even the most extraordinary and wildest dreams into reality. It might sound far-fetched to many, but if history is any guide, things that were once considered pure fantasy have often become an integral part of our lives. Who would have thought a century ago that we'd be able to video call people from across the globe for free or have tiny computers in our pockets?

We're on the brink of a future filled with endless possibilities. Our understanding of science and technology is just beginning. What we know now might be a mere fraction of what's to come. For all we know, we could be at the tip of an enormous iceberg of discoveries.

Science fiction writer Arthur C. Clarke formulated three adages that are known as Clarke's three laws, of which the third law is the best known and most widely cited.[1] They are part of his ideas in his extensive writings about the future. The laws are:

- When a distinguished but elderly scientist states that something is possible, they are almost certainly right. When they state that something is impossible, they are very probably wrong.
- The only way of discovering the limits of the possible is to venture a little way past them into the impossible.
- Any sufficiently advanced technology is indistinguishable from magic.

Clarke's words remind us that the boundaries between the impossible and the achievable are constantly shifting. So, what does this mean for the future we're building? Keep dreaming big, stay curious, and always ask where we're going. Our imagination is a powerful tool for sparking progress and envisioning a future that exceeds our wildest dreams. After all, as Clarke pointed out, today's impossibilities might be tomorrow's reality.

I'm speaking to the future's builders—all of us. Whether we like it or not, we're all part of creating what's to come, through our actions or our words. Embracing change and seeing its potential is the first step in making progress. It begins with recognizing the full potential and not just following others' views. But, do we recognize its full potential? How do we measure the success of technology in our economy? Are we using the right metrics to appreciate technology and keep improving? These are the questions I aim to address in this chapter.

REALITY CHECK: DIGITAL HAPPINESS

In an era characterized by rapid technological advancements, the digital realm often finds itself at the epicenter of both praise and criticism. Many, especially technology experts and scholars, frequently express concerns over the potential negative impacts of technology on various facets of life—be it social, political, or economic. Yet, it's noteworthy that these same experts typically confess to having a largely positive personal experience with digital life. This dichotomy begs the question: how do we recognize the real contribution of digital tools and technology to happiness?

Nevertheless, embracing digital tools isn't without its challenges. It took me four years to carve out my identity on Instagram and other social platforms, to navigate the chaos and discover my authentic message. The struggle and the growth—it's a familiar path for those finding their place online. Feeling anxious or overwhelmed is a normal part of getting used to new technology. But by sticking with it and learning good digital habits, we can use these tools to help us find happiness.

From my perspective, the magic of technology lies not in a universal narrative of happiness but in its ability to unlock opportunities for a diverse range of individuals. Consider this: while it's tempting to think of technology as a leveler for the less fortunate, its power to open doors extends far beyond financial barriers. Even those with limited resources can find themselves excluded from opportunities, until technology offers a key. Take, for example, the story of a small-town artist. With no galleries to showcase her work, she turns to social media, sharing her art online. Soon, her creations catch the eye of an international audience, catapulting her into a world that once seemed out of reach. Think about how we can talk to someone on the other side of the world with just a click or how we can enjoy movies and music anytime. Doctors use cool gadgets to help us stay healthy, and new inventions keep our planet clean and safe. All these things from technology can make us smile and feel good.

Echoing physicist and mathematician Freeman Dyson's sentiment, "Technology is a gift of God. After the gift of life it is perhaps the greatest of God's gifts. It is the mother of civilizations, of arts and of sciences," technology is like a special present, right after the gift of being alive. It helps build our communities, makes art more creative, and pushes science to learn new things. It's a big reason why our lives keep getting better.

BEYOND THE GROSS DOMESTIC PRODUCT (GDP): THE GROSS NATIONAL HAPPINESS (GNH)

Technology is changing our lives a lot. In their book *The Second Machine Age*, Brynjolfsson and McAfee talk about why the way we usually measure a country's success, with something called GDP, isn't enough anymore. GDP is like a score that tells us how many goods and services a country is producing and selling. But this score doesn't show everything about how people are living and if they're happy.

Think about when kids laugh and play, or when we all learn something new that makes us go, "Wow!" These things make life better, but they don't show up in the GDP score. And even though we spend money on schools and hospitals, GDP doesn't tell us if the education is really good or if everyone is feeling healthy and strong.

Now, what about having fun and relaxing, or enjoying music, movies, and art? Or how strong our friendships and families are? These are really important for a good life, but you can't see them in the GDP numbers. Also, being able to trust what's on the news and that the people in charge are doing a good job is super important, but again, not something GDP can tell us.

Let us ponder the health of our children. GDP accounts for healthcare spending but remains silent on the vitality and laughter of our youth. It says nothing of the children whose days are brightened by innovative educational apps, whose well-being is preserved by telemedicine, or whose creativity is sparked by interactive, digital learning platforms.

Consider the quality of education. Here, we invest in institutions, but GDP fails to capture the true essence of learning: the joy of a student's "aha" moment, the ease of access to global knowledge databases, or the silent thanksgiving of a parent witnessing their child conquer a challenging concept via an online tutoring session—all fruits of our technological era.

Then there's the joy of play—an integral part of human happiness. GDP does not account for the leisure hours saved through smart home devices or the enjoyment of connecting with friends via online gaming platforms. It disregards the joy of virtual reality, where we can share experiences and go beyond what's physically possible.

What of the beauty of poetry and the arts? GDP may include the transaction value of a sold painting, but it ignores the shared cultural heritage preserved through digital archives, the communal joy felt when streaming a concert in live 360-degree video, or the personal solace found in creating digital art on a tablet.

The strength of marriages and relationships, too, is omitted from this economic measure. Yet, technology facilitates connections through communication tools that bridge distances, providing platforms for shared experiences and support systems that reinforce the bonds of love and friendship, which are essential for well-being.

Furthermore, GDP does not reflect the quality of public debate or the integrity of public officials. Yet, the Digital Age has democratized information, giving rise to citizen journalism and social media campaigns that hold leaders accountable and invigorate public discourse.

And what of wit, courage, wisdom, learning, compassion, and devotion? These attributes of a thriving society are nowhere to be found in the cold calculations of GDP. Yet, they are nurtured by the vast information networks and collaborative technologies that underpin our modern society, fostering a global community that learns from shared experiences and collective wisdom.

Robert F. Kennedy once said something that helps explain this. In a speech on March 18, 1968, he said:

> The gross national product does not allow for the health of our children, the quality of their education, or the joy of their play. It does not include the beauty of our poetry or the strength of our marriages; the intelligence of our public debate or the integrity of our public officials ... It measures neither our wit nor our courage; neither our wisdom nor our learning; neither our compassion nor our devotion to our country; it

measures everything, in short, except that which makes
life worthwhile.

Kennedy's words are even more important now that technology is such
a big part of our lives. He knew that what really matters—like how we
take care of our kids, enjoy our free time, and appreciate things like art
and nature—doesn't show up in the GDP score.

It's clear that while technology's contributions to happiness and progress
are vast, they are not always captured by traditional economic indicators
like GDP. This suggests the need for developing new metrics that can
more accurately reflect the technological benefits to society's happiness
and well-being.

This is where Gross National Happiness (GNH), as conceptualized
by Bhutan's fourth Dragon King, Jigme Singye Wangchuck,[2] enters the
conversation. GNH seeks to quantify the unquantifiable, measuring
the well-being of a society not just by its economic output, but by the
happiness and satisfaction of its people. It is a philosophy that aligns
with the views of Kennedy and the insights of Brynjolfsson and McAfee,
highlighting the need for metrics that value health, education, the
environment, and cultural richness as integral facets of societal success.

In conclusion, as we embrace the second machine age, we must expand
our measures of progress. We need to go beyond GDP, to see the fabric
of society through a lens that captures the vibrancy of human life
enriched by technology. Kennedy's call to look beyond mere economic
metrics finds its answer in the philosophy of GNH and in our collective
pursuit of a happiness that is as intricate and multifaceted as the human
experience itself. In this digital epoch, our challenge is to craft a narrative
of progress that harmonizes the rhythm of economic growth with the
melody of human joy, ensuring that as we advance, we do so not just
in wealth, but in well-being. As we navigate this journey, our aim is to
become truly more alive, ultimately leading to human transcendence,
and fully engage with the transformative power of technology in
enhancing every aspect of our existence.

SMART CITIES AS TESTBEDS FOR GROSS NATIONAL HAPPINESS (GNH) MEASUREMENT

Beyond their direct contributions to GDP, smart cities offer an unprecedented opportunity to test and measure the principles of Gross National Happiness. The interconnected nature of smart city systems provides a unique environment to quantify how technology impacts factors like well-being, education, cultural experiences, and community engagement. For example, a smart city might feature sensors tracking air quality and pollution levels that can correlate with health outcomes, providing data to assess how technology contributes to the physical environment. Similarly, analyzing traffic patterns and public transportation usage could reveal how efficient urban planning impacts citizens' leisure time and sense of ease within their cities. Smart city platforms can also facilitate cultural experiences: tracking attendance at museums, offering virtual tours, or promoting participation in online arts programs. These metrics, often difficult to capture in traditional settings, become tangible within the data-rich landscape of a smart city.

Furthermore, smart city technologies can foster a stronger sense of community. Communication platforms and citizen feedback systems provide channels for residents to voice their opinions, participate in decision-making, and feel a sense of ownership over their urban environment. This active engagement can contribute to greater citizen satisfaction and a sense of belonging, both integral aspects of Gross National Happiness.

By utilizing these technologies, smart cities can become testbeds for understanding the complex relationship between innovation, economic progress, and the multifaceted nature of human happiness. The data gathered can inform policy decisions, ensuring that investments in technology simultaneously boost GDP and enhance those intangible yet essential elements that make life truly fulfilling. This approach aligns with the philosophy that a city's success is not just measured in economic output, but in the happiness and well-being of its people. Smart cities, with their emphasis on efficiency, sustainability, and citizen-centric design, embody the potential to reconcile the pursuit of economic growth with the human desire for connection, meaning, and a thriving community. Ultimately, they offer a blueprint for building urban environments where progress is measured not just by numbers on a spreadsheet, but by the collective well-being of those who call them home.

Already, urban areas contribute approximately 80% of the global GDP, a figure that is expected to rise as cities become smarter and more efficient.[3] The integration of technology in the urban setting directly correlates with increased productivity and economic diversification.[4]

The futuristic vision of projects like Neom in Saudi Arabia is a case in point. Here, cutting-edge technology meets sustainable living, creating a synergy that is anticipated to fuel an unprecedented economic surge. It's a city that aspires to be an ecosystem of prosperity, a place where the economy flourishes alongside nature and technology.

The economic experiment that is Neom transcends traditional metrics; it embodies the ambition to carve out a significant share of the country's economic narrative. Once operational, its contribution to the GDP isn't just expected to be substantial—it's forecasted to be transformative, marking a new chapter in how cities can amplify a nation's economic vitality and international standing.

Beyond GDP, Neom presents an opportunity to test and measure Gross National Happiness (GNH) principles. Its interconnected smart systems can quantify citizen well-being, track environmental impact, and assess community engagement. It can become a living laboratory for understanding how technology, urban design, and social policies interact to create a society where economic progress and human flourishing go hand-in-hand.

In the context of well-being, the prosperity engendered by smart cities is not just measured in economic terms but also in the enhanced quality of life they offer. The gains in efficiency, health, education, and connectivity foster an environment where well-being and productivity reinforce each other. When citizens thrive, their productivity increases, further stimulating economic growth.

As smart cities evolve, the intricacy of their contribution to national and global GDP becomes multifaceted. The direct economic output from industries and services is bolstered by the secondary effects of enhanced well-being and the tertiary effects of innovation and intellectual property generated within their precincts.

In crafting the urban landscapes of tomorrow, city planners and policymakers must weave together technology, policy, and citizen engagement to create an urban tapestry that reflects the collective ambition for a society where economic growth and human well-being are in synergy, demonstrating that our most complex "products"—our cities—can indeed be our most prosperous and life-enhancing creations.

TECH-ENABLED PREVENTION FOR SMARTER LIVES

Who wouldn't yearn for immediate medical attention and the unparalleled capability to proactively prevent severe health conditions? This is the essence of the Smart Lives philosophy—leveraging technology to empower individuals to take control of their health, improve their quality of life, and potentially reduce the overall burden on healthcare systems. However, gaps and disparities in healthcare persist globally. Some countries place healthcare on the backburner, deeming it less critical, while nations like Switzerland (first), Ireland (second), the Netherlands (third), and Germany (fourth) are fervently propelling it forward. As evidenced by the 2022 World Index of Healthcare Innovation (WIHI), these nations top the ranks.[5] The WIHI meticulously employs data to rank healthcare systems across 32 countries, assessing them on four paramount dimensions: quality, choice, science and technology, and fiscal sustainability. Such an emphasis on innovation yields palpable results: the mortality rates in these top-ranking countries remain conspicuously lower than the global norm. But innovation isn't just about developing cutting-edge treatments; it's also about widespread access, efficiency, and affordability of care.

The United States is a titan when it comes to healthcare research expenditure. With an impressive allocation of nearly $245.1 billion in 2020, it dwarfs other nations in this arena.[6] This colossal investment translates to breakthroughs in drug development, treatment modalities, and innovative care pathways. Home to a wide array of world-renowned medical institutions, the US has been a cradle for medical innovation.

Research and development (R&D) in healthcare is not just an expense; it's a visionary commitment to the future. Nations at the pinnacle of healthcare advancements are invariably those that heavily channel resources into healthcare research. Their unwavering focus on innovation heralds not just medical breakthroughs but also optimizes patient care and experiences.

While factors such as lifestyle, diet, and environmental conditions significantly influence a country's health metrics, we cannot dismiss the profound impact of healthcare innovation on mortality rates. A pivotal study published in *Nature Medicine* underscores this relationship, asserting that healthcare innovation correlates with reduced mortality rates, even when considering confounding factors like GDP per capita or healthcare expenditure.[7] Leading the charge in this regard are countries like Switzerland, the Netherlands, Germany, Sweden, Ireland, Japan, and South Korea. Their consistent performance in healthcare innovation indexes parallels their commendable mortality rates.

Historical perspectives provide an insightful context. The past 50 years have witnessed monumental advancements in healthcare, translating into a tangible enhancement in the global standard of living. Eminent research, such as a study undertaken by William Nordhaus[8] as well as another study by Kevin Murphy and Robert Topel,[9] have underscored the substantial socio-economic benefits stemming from increased longevity. These improvements are the culmination of a broad spectrum of factors, from revamped public infrastructure to the advent of state-of-the-art medical practices and awareness. And to advance the frontiers of longevity research, it's important to consider partnerships and collaborations between private and public sectors.

There are many private sector entities that are eager to explore this domain. For example, in 2018, the CEO of Spotify, Daniel Ek, co-founded a startup, Neko Health, along with Hjalmar Nilsonne, a Swedish health-tech trailblazer who is at the vanguard of reimagining healthcare for the modern age. Neko Health's mission is nothing short of transformative: to usher in a healthcare system rooted in preventive care and early detection. Its groundbreaking medical scanning technology offers broad, non-invasive health data collection that's both accessible and economical for the masses.

The centerpiece of Neko's innovative offerings is the Neko Body Scan. This state-of-the-art diagnostic tool encompasses a comprehensive array of tests capable of detecting a wide range of health conditions— ranging from skin cancer and cardiovascular diseases to diabetes. Each scan, taking a mere ten minutes, culminates in a thorough consultation with a medical professional, ensuring patients are not just informed, but also guided.

In the realm of healthcare, groundbreaking advancements often emerge from the confluence of individual innovation and collaborative synergy. A prime example of this is the collaboration between the UK's National Health Service (NHS) and DeepMind, a subsidiary of tech giant Google. Together, they've embarked on a journey to harness the power of AI-driven algorithms and mobile tools, equipping healthcare professionals with state-of-the-art solutions.

A flagship project under this collaboration has been the early detection and prevention of acute kidney injuries. The fruits of their alliance are manifold: not only have they set new standards in integrating tech innovation with state healthcare infrastructure, but they've also ushered in substantial financial savings for the NHS.

A pivotal study showcased in the Lancet in 2020 underscores this, revealing that the Streams algorithm, a brainchild of this partnership, curtailed the need for dialysis in patients by a remarkable 17%.[10] Through such transformative collaborations, the horizon of healthcare is being redrawn, steering us towards an era characterized by proactive, predictive, and bespoke medical care.

However, these advancements don't come without challenges. The looming shadow of data security concerns, the imperative for continuous upskilling of healthcare personnel, and the quest for access equity represent significant hurdles. Ensuring that everyone, regardless of their socio-economic standing, can avail top-notch care remains a challenge. In the subsequent chapters, we'll delve deeper into these challenges, understanding their roots and exploring potential solutions.

PATH FORWARD

The true meaning of progress lies beyond the narrow focus on economic growth as captured by GDP. As we harness the power of technology, we must shape a future where human well-being and our planet's health are paramount, not solely a relentless pursuit of profit.

As we forge this path, it is essential to develop new frameworks for measuring success. These frameworks must incorporate factors such as well-being, environmental integrity, and social cohesion. They should capture the full breadth of human experience, from the health of our families and communities to the vibrancy of our cultures and the resilience of our ecosystems.

Nations must boldly invest in the creation of cognitive cities and smart cities. These urban environments will serve as living laboratories, where we can test, refine, and scale technologies that enhance the lives of citizens. Priority sectors for development include:

- *Education (Including R&D)*: pioneering a transformative educational model. Smart cities can be incubators for revolutionizing not just how we teach, but what we teach. Policymakers and educators must challenge traditional curricula, years of study, and teaching methodologies with a focus on future-ready skills and adaptability. We need to drive innovation through robust R&D funding, incentivizing experimentation and attracting the world's brightest minds to create a scalable blueprint for the future of education. This mirrors initiatives seen globally as cities adapt to the demands of the future. In South Korea's Songdo International Business District, smart city development prioritizes knowledge creation by attracting leading universities and fostering collaboration. Meanwhile, Espoo in Finland emphasizes personalized learning, technology integration, and collaborative learning environments for lifelong learning within their smart city framework.
- *Healthcare*: reimagining medicine for the 21st century. Smart cities offer fertile ground for a complete overhaul of healthcare, from proactive prevention to personalized, data-fueled treatment. Government and industry leaders must prioritize heavy R&D investment in areas like AI-driven diagnostics, gene editing, and regenerative medicine. They should foster a collaborative ecosystem where medical professionals, researchers, and technologists work seamlessly to accelerate breakthroughs and optimize outcomes for patients.
- *Security/Privacy/Safety*: building future-proof security and privacy infrastructure. Smart cities demand a paradigm shift in how we protect citizens and their data. Smart city planners and security experts must develop cutting-edge cybersecurity systems that instill trust while leveraging data for the common good. Simultaneously, they should enhance physical safety

through smart infrastructure, predictive policing models, and community-integrated safety systems.

This journey requires collaborative efforts across different fields of expertise. Only through cross-disciplinary cooperation can we balance the impressive power of digital technologies with a firm commitment to ethical principles. By integrating insights from science, humanities, policymaking, and beyond, we can steer the digital revolution towards a future where technology acts as a catalyst for comprehensive societal prosperity, not just as a driver of economic metrics.

Our resolve must be to ensure that technology serves as a tool for crafting a society that is more equitable, just, and fulfilling. This is the challenge of our time, and it is one that we must meet with creativity, determination, and an unwavering dedication to the common good.

As we conclude our exploration of how smart cities and cognitive urban environments can enhance human well-being and environmental health, we recognize that these technological advancements are only part of the broader digital experience that shapes our lives. The same innovative spirit that drives the development of these cities also permeates our personal digital interactions, which brings us to a crucial juncture.

Chapter 4, "The Subtle Art of Algorithmic Influence" shifts our focus from the macro impact of technology on cities and societies to the micro impacts on individual mental health and social behaviors. Our digital lives, while offering unprecedented connectivity and access to information, also come with significant challenges. Algorithms designed to captivate our attention often lead to shorter attention spans, increased anxiety, and a sense of overwhelm. Even as technology creators are aware of these issues, the imperative to drive profit often overshadows the need for ethical considerations. In the next chapter we will explore the responsibility of tech creators and the actions we can take to reclaim agency and promote a more mindful use of the digital tools at our disposal.

CHAPTER 3 TAKEAWAYS

The way we measure societal progress is changing. GDP, focused on economic output, doesn't reflect the full impact of technology on happiness and well-being.

To better track societal success, we can look to Bhutan's philosophy of Gross National Happiness (GNH). This emphasizes well-being, education, the environment, and cultural preservation over purely economic metrics.

Smart cities are perfect testbeds for GNH. Their systems let us track how tech affects well-being, education, community, and cultural experiences. This data can guide policy for cities where progress is defined by people's happiness, not just economic growth.

Healthcare is another area where the impact of technology is immense. Smart health initiatives use tech for prevention and early detection, improving quality of life and saving money. But challenges like data security, skills updates, and ensuring access for all need to be addressed.

THE SUBTLE ART OF ALGORITHMIC INFLUENCE

Algorithms are the newest tool for manufacturing consent.
By deciphering their methods, we resist becoming unwitting
participants in our own digital conditioning.

—Noam Chomsky

Reflect for a moment—when you first navigated the landscape of social media, were you aware of the algorithms working silently behind each click, each post, and every digital interaction? I certainly wasn't. It wasn't until around 2020 that I, along with many others, began to realize this. It's fascinating, isn't it? The way these algorithms operate in the shadows, subtly influencing our daily digital experiences.

I remember chatting with a friend about a niche product, only to find ads for that very item popping up on my social feeds. It felt like a coincidence at first, but as this pattern repeated, it became clear that there was something more at play. It was as if Facebook and Instagram were eavesdropping on my conversations. The thought was both intriguing and unsettling.

Think about it: when you search for something online, say a wedding planner one day and wedding shoes the next, you're not just passing time—you're providing valuable information about yourself. You're giving these platforms a peek into your life, your plans, your preferences. Soon, they know what you're looking for even before you do. Your digital feed transforms into a personalized storefront, tailored to your tastes and needs. It's convenient, no doubt. You find things you never knew you wanted. But it's also slightly disturbing. These algorithms don't just understand your preferences; they start shaping your choices, nudging you towards decisions you might not have made independently.

It begs the question: is this truly a new phenomenon, unique to our Digital Age? Or does it echo the way we, as consumers, have always behaved? I often ponder this, especially when I think back to my younger days, accompanying my mother on shopping trips. We'd have a list, a plan. But more often than not, we'd deviate. A skilled salesperson's suggestion, an eye-catching display, or even just a whim could sway our decisions. Sometimes, we'd leave loaded with unexpected purchases. Other times, we'd return home empty-handed, the offerings not quite what we imagined.

In essence, our behavior hasn't changed drastically. Just like the busy marketplaces of old, where vendors observed and pitched diverse wares, today's online world seeks to tempt us. Facebook and Instagram aim to become digital marketplaces, full of options tailored to our perceived desires. Technology transforms the context, but the underlying principles of economic exchange remain surprisingly familiar. The essence of commerce and consumer interaction remains constant; it's the medium that has evolved.

However, with this evolution comes a downside. Our online interactions, preferences, decisions—they're all being captured, analyzed, and stored. This vast repository of personal data, a concept once confined to the realms of science fiction, is now an everyday reality. It's not just about targeted advertising anymore. The implications stretch further. The data can be, and sometimes is, used in ways we never intended. Consider the implications for privacy, for autonomy, for freedom of choice.

There's a subtle yet significant shift in the dynamics of power and knowledge. These algorithms, fed by our data, seem to know us better than we know ourselves. They predict our needs, our desires, sometimes even before we can articulate them. After all, they have more perspective on our behavior than we do. It's not magic—we often act without fully understanding our own motivations. But by tracking and analyzing our data, these algorithms can uncover those patterns and reveal insights we might miss on our own.

As we progress through this chapter, I aim to guide you towards a deeper understanding of our relationship with the algorithms that have become an integral part of our digital lives. We'll explore not only how these algorithms operate and their impact on our decision-making, but most importantly delve into ways we can exert control over them. The focus will shift towards how we can shape our digital identities and maintain our privacy in this interconnected realm.

This journey is about empowerment. It's about understanding how we, as individuals, can protect ourselves, forge a harmonious relationship with these algorithms, and turn a system that often feels invasive into something beneficial. Instead of simply being passive consumers of technology, we have the potential to be active participants, influencing and countering the system to work in our favor.

We'll tackle questions like: how do we maintain our autonomy in a world where our choices may be subtly influenced by the underlying code? How can we manage our digital footprint in a way that respects our privacy yet allows us to enjoy the conveniences of modern technology? Can we become "friends" with the algorithm, understanding its workings well enough to make it serve us rather than manipulate us?

ENSLAVED BY THE ALGORITHM

In this digital era, our lives are deeply connected to social media and online platforms. It's a tapestry that, while rich and vibrant, also presents a complex array of challenges and repercussions that are worth exploring in depth.

At the core of our interaction with these platforms is a subtle yet profound loss of focus and control. A study by Microsoft found that since the year 2000 (or about when the mobile revolution began) the average attention span dropped from 12 seconds to eight seconds.[1] The study suggests that constant exposure to multiple media streams makes it harder to filter out distractions and maintain focus. However, we've become significantly better at multitasking within the digital world. Microsoft theorized that the changes were a result of the brain's ability to adapt and change itself over time and a weaker attention span may be a side effect of evolving to a mobile internet.

This shift points to a broader trend where the constant influx of information from social media platforms and news apps overwhelms and fragments our concentration. The design of these platforms, with their endless scrolls and streams of content, is engineered to capture and hold our attention, often at the expense of deeper, more focused thinking.

The contradiction is clear—in seeking to stay informed and connected, we may be nurturing a form of a digitally distracted mind, hopping from one piece of content to another without fully engaging with any.

But perhaps one of the most profound effects of this algorithmic engagement is on our choices and decisions. The alteration in our decision-making processes due to algorithmic influence is equally significant. The filter bubbles created by these algorithms are not just about reaffirming our views; they also shape our choices, often without our conscious awareness. A study from the Pew Research Center shows that about half of Americans get their news from social media, where what they see is largely determined by algorithms.[2] This mode of information consumption can limit exposure to diverse perspectives and challenge the very foundations of a well-informed, democratic society.

The algorithms curating our digital experiences are designed to present us with content that aligns with our past behavior and preferences. While this might seem beneficial, it also runs the risk of narrowing our worldviews. The concept of filter bubbles, as introduced by internet activist Eli Pariser, illustrates this well.[3] These bubbles encapsulate us in a digital echo chamber, reinforcing our existing beliefs and shielding us from contrasting perspectives. This phenomenon isn't just limited to our social interactions but extends to how we consume news, form opinions, and make decisions, potentially leading to a more polarized society.

The implications of these filter bubbles are far-reaching. In the realm of politics, for example, the way news is consumed on these platforms can profoundly affect public opinion. For example, a study published in the National Center for Biotechnology Information (NCBI) found that algorithms could influence voting patterns, demonstrating the power they wield over public discourse and democracy.[4] The study results showed that Facebook messages influenced political self-expression and voting behavior in millions of people, thus a testament to the power they have over public discourse and democracy.

Another layer to this complex picture is the impact on mental health. The constant exposure to idealized versions of reality on platforms like Instagram has been linked to rising rates of anxiety and depression, particularly among young adults.[5] This digital landscape, with its curated realities, often leads to unfair comparisons and a perpetual sense of falling short, contributing to a societal undercurrent of discontent and self-doubt.

Moreover, the addictive nature of these platforms cannot be underestimated. Designed to hook users with mechanisms similar to those used in gambling, such as variable rewards, they create patterns of dependency. This addiction not only impacts mental well-being but also productivity and real-life interactions. It's a paradox of connection—as we become more connected online, there's a risk of becoming more disconnected in the real world, from our immediate surroundings and physical relationships.

Perhaps one of the most disturbing consequences of this digital integration is the proliferation of misinformation. The same algorithms that help us find content we like are also adept at spreading misinformation. A study by MIT researchers found that false news spreads more rapidly on Twitter than real news does.[6] Falsehoods are 70% more likely to be retweeted on Twitter than the truth, researchers found. And false news reached 1,500 people about six times faster than the truth. This phenomenon is not just a matter of public misinformation but can have serious consequences, influencing everything from stock markets to political elections.

Pause for a moment to consider this: despite the technological marvels surrounding us, people today—particularly those in Gen Y (millennials) and Z—are deeply affected by stress and overwhelm. As we will dissect in Chapter 6, these feelings are not without cause. To put it into perspective, a recent study from Deloitte reveals the vast majority of Gen Zs (87%) and millennials (80%) use social media to consume news, looking to friends and family on these channels as a top source above national news providers.[7] The constant flow of information from social media and from a 24-hour news cycle likely adds to stress levels. More than six in ten Gen Zs (63%) and millennials (61%) say they frequently or occasionally limit their exposure to news and current affairs to protect their mental health.

This, in essence, sheds light on their frequent retreat into the world of smartphones, entertainment, and social media—a way to escape the pressures of the real world. Recognizing this as a normal response to the stresses they face is important.

Yet, the story changes when we consider the people who create these digital spaces. Figures like Mark Zuckerberg, the minds behind our screens, must realize that their creations are more than mere platforms; they are places where a generation seeks comfort. The ethical dilemma is clear: rather than using this need to trap users in an endless cycle of meaningless content, there's a great opportunity to focus on support and growth. We're talking about rethinking algorithms—not as tools to capture attention, but as ways to inform and inspire. This brings us to a dual-faceted solution:

1. *Creator Responsibility—Ethical Algorithm Design*: for the architects and creators of our digital experiences, the call to action is clear. The design of algorithms must transcend the pursuit of profit and user engagement to prioritize the mental and emotional health of users. This shift entails crafting algorithms that foster meaningful interactions, promote mental well-being, and serve as gateways to educational and enriching content. It's a journey from profit-driven motives to a paradigm where user welfare is the cornerstone of success.

2. *User Mindfulness—Befriending the Algorithm*: it's imperative to arm the younger generation with the knowledge and skills to navigate the digital landscape wisely. This involves cultivating a deep understanding of how these algorithms operate and how they can be harnessed for personal growth and well-being.

It's about transforming users from passive consumers into informed navigators of the digital world.

Embarking on this path, we can forge a digital ecosystem that not only respects but nurtures the mental and emotional well-being of the younger generations, steering them towards a more enlightened and fulfilling digital future. In doing so, we empower them to be more "alive," fully engaged and enriched by every experience, embodying the essence of our goal to "die alive."

CREATOR RESPONSIBILITY— ETHICAL ALGORITHM DESIGN

The way I currently perceive creators of digital platforms is predominantly as capitalist kingpins and data monetizers, intently focused on leveraging our data and every insight we provide for financial gain. But here's an intriguing proposition for these astute business minds: what if you could achieve, or perhaps even double, your financial returns by shifting your focus? It's about considering what people truly need, not just what you need from them.

This approach goes beyond transactional interactions. It's about redefining the value proposition of digital platforms, where understanding and catering to the genuine needs of users could lead to greater engagement, loyalty, and ultimately, profitability. In an era where the user is more discerning and informed than ever, aligning platform goals with user needs is not just ethical but could also be a more effective business strategy.

Enter Generation Z, a demographic challenging every established norm, building new realities, and passionately desiring meaningful contributions. This generation doesn't just consume; they create, question, and innovate. So, why not support them instead of anchoring them in outdated paradigms that slow down the evolution of ideas?

For the creators and custodians of our digital realms, the path forward is illuminated with clarity. The algorithms, the very foundation of these platforms, must evolve beyond the narrow confines of profit and user engagement metrics. They should aim to prioritize the mental and emotional well-being of their users. It's about crafting algorithms that don't just captivate but enlighten; that don't merely entertain but educate and enrich. This isn't just a shift in technology; it's a renaissance in the guiding principles that support digital innovation. Herein lies the promise of not just maintaining but potentially doubling your gains—by aligning with the needs and aspirations of a generation that values substance over superficiality. This approach redefines success, not in financial terms, but as a measure of the positive impact on the lives of users. We need to encourage new startups to apply this mindset, fostering a new wave of digital innovation that serves humanity.

USER MINDFULNESS—BEFRIENDING THE ALGORITHM

In our Digital Age, algorithms have become ubiquitous, subtly shaping our online experiences and decisions. The profound question that arises is whether we can become "friends" with these algorithms, understanding their workings well enough to make them serve us, rather than manipulate us. This exploration is not merely a technical endeavor but a journey into the heart of our interaction with the digital world.

Just as understanding a friend requires comprehension of their language and motivations, so does befriending an algorithm. Algorithms are essentially data-driven entities, analyzing patterns in our behavior to predict and influence our actions. This understanding is critical because, unlike human interactions where mutual benefit is often the goal, an algorithm's primary aim may be centered around engagement and profit. The algorithm is designed to serve us, and without our inputs it cannot function. Recognizing this underlying motive is crucial in navigating our relationship with them.

To forge a beneficial relationship with algorithms, we need first transparency from the platforms that use them. This transparency is about knowing how our data is used and understanding the decisions these algorithms make on our behalf. It's comparable to trust in human relationships—knowing the "why" behind actions builds a foundation for healthy interaction.

Algorithms evolve based on user interaction. This means we have the power to shape these algorithms through our online behavior. Consciously engaging with content that aligns with our interests and values, and avoiding what doesn't, sends clear signals to the algorithm, training it to cater to our preferences. This process is similar to setting boundaries in a friendship, where we reinforce behaviors that resonate with us and discourage those that don't.

As we delve deeper into this relationship, it's crucial to explore strategies that can foster a more harmonious interaction with these digital platforms, so let's do that.

In our era of digital abundance, conscious consumption is a beacon of self-guidance. This strategy revolves around making informed choices in our online interactions to guide the algorithm's understanding of our preferences. Our lives are in constant flux; within a single year, perspectives can shift and needs evolve across multiple areas of our lives. For this reason, it's essential to regularly refresh our purpose. Just as with our real-world choices, our online consumption can become stale if it doesn't adapt to our current purpose. Many users find themselves trapped in a content "echo chamber," with their feeds becoming a mirror of their past views that has not been refreshed. By intentionally diversifying our viewing habits, we can steer the algorithm towards suggesting a broader content spectrum. This shift breaks the monotony of similar content and exposes users to new perspectives and ideas.

Let's delve into a concept that's often overlooked in our Digital Age: purposeful engagement with social media platforms. Take Instagram, for instance. I recall a pivotal moment when I consciously decided the nature of my interactions on this platform. My strategy? A deliberate focus. I chose to share once or twice a week stories about my personal life and opinions—a practice that not only keeps my friends updated on my life's happenings but also fosters regular interaction. It's a balanced approach, offering a window into my world without giving in to the pressures of overexposure.

The real transformation, however, came in how I engaged with content on Instagram. There was a time when I realized, somewhat surprisingly, that I was spending upwards of three hours daily, aimlessly scrolling through stories, often leading to impulsive shopping decisions. This was a wake-up call. How could I reshape Instagram into a tool for enlightenment rather than a black hole of time wastage?

With my focus pivoting to personal development, I deliberately unfollowed influencers fixated on makeup and outfits, whose content no longer resonated with my goals. Simultaneously, I began seeking out accounts driven by business insights, personal growth, and even emerging areas like Web3. This strategic curation had a profound impact: when I now open Instagram, my feed is filled with content related to my interests. This shift not only refined the quality of content I consumed but also dramatically reduced my daily usage time from three hours to a mere 30 minutes. It's a testament to the power of intentional digital engagement—reshaping a platform from a distraction into a source of valuable learning and growth.

This is a compelling example of how we can reclaim control over our digital experiences, steering them towards our personal aspirations and learning goals. It's about transforming platforms from mere pastimes into potent tools for self-improvement and knowledge acquisition.

In our current digital landscape, where information is unending and our attention is constantly in demand, mastering the art of conscious digital consumption becomes crucial. This approach isn't just about selective content engagement; it's a holistic strategy for managing our digital lives.

The core of this philosophy is to use digital tools in a way that enhances our well-being, rather than allowing them to overwhelm or distract us. Conscious consumption, in this context, means taking proactive steps to ensure that our interaction with technology aligns with our personal goals, values, and mental health. It's about creating a digital experience that supports our lifestyle, rather than detracting from it.

This perspective is vital when considering the impact of digital platforms on our daily lives. For instance, consider how easily we can get caught up in a cycle of excessive screen time, leading to digital fatigue and a disconnect from the physical world. By employing mindful strategies, we can prevent such pitfalls and ensure that our technology use is both meaningful and balanced.

Now, to illustrate this with personal examples:

> *Defining Your Purpose in Digital Platforms:* before diving into any platform, take a moment to write down what you want to get out of it. Are you looking for entertainment, news, connection with friends, or something else? Having this clarity will help you focus your engagement, and it's easy to revisit your purpose if your needs shift.

> *Setting Usage Limits on Platforms*: on my phone, I have configured specific time limits for each social media platform. When I reach this limit, a notification prompts me to disengage. This simple but effective method keeps my digital engagement in check, ensuring that I don't spend an excessive amount of time on these platforms.

> *Conscious Curation of Notifications*: I made a conscious choice to mute all non-essential notifications. This decision significantly reduced distractions and decreased my overall screen time. By limiting these

constant digital interruptions, I found that my phone became less of an incessant demand for attention and more of a purposeful tool.

These strategies have helped me reshape my digital habits, but it's important to remember that they're not a one-time solution. Our needs and the platforms themselves will evolve. Regardless of the leading platform, let's always dedicate at least ten to 15 minutes to understand what it offers, how it works, and the implications for ourselves and our children.

PATH FORWARD: EDUCATIONAL EMPOWERMENT

In today's complex digital world, knowledge truly is power, particularly when it comes to understanding and navigating the algorithms that shape our digital interactions. With the rise of online platforms, algorithms have become the invisible architects of our digital experiences. Recognizing their influence, there's a growing movement towards demystifying these complex systems. Many online courses, webinars, and resources are now available to help people understand how algorithms work. These tools are not just academic exercises; they are empowering instruments for the everyday user. By learning about algorithmic biases and operation, individuals can navigate the digital realm with increased awareness and discernment.

Consider, for example, the Data Detox Kit, an initiative created by a non-profit organization focused on the intersection of technology and human rights. It provides a set of resources designed to help a person take control of their digital life and improve their online experiences. It's a vital resource in an era where understanding the interplay between data and algorithms is becoming a necessary skill. By comprehending how algorithms interpret our data and actions, we're better equipped to steer our online experiences in directions that align with our preferences and privacy concerns.

The way we interact with digital platforms holds significant influence over how algorithms evolve. User feedback mechanisms on social media platforms exemplify this. By engaging with these systems—be it through participating in user surveys, beta testing new features, or utilizing direct feedback channels—we don't just passively consume content; we actively shape a platform's evolution. This engagement ensures that the platform evolves to better cater to user needs and preferences, fostering a more user-centric digital environment.

Beyond individual efforts, there's a profound impact to be found in collective action. Online forums and communities, like Reddit's r/privacy, have become crucial in this regard. They provide spaces where users can share insights, strategies, and experiences related to managing algorithmic interactions. These communal dialogues offer a plethora of perspectives and solutions, contributing to a richer individual understanding and more potent collective action.

In the realm of content curation by algorithms, fostering critical thinking becomes paramount. Take the News Literacy Project, created by an American non-profit organization dedicated to teaching middle and high school students how to discern fact from fiction in the Digital Age. This platform provides educators with free resources, including lesson plans, activities, and professional development, to help them integrate news literacy into their classrooms, so they can equip students with the skills needed to scrutinize and evaluate the information presented to them.

In an era rife with misinformation, this ability to assess the credibility of online content is more crucial than ever. It's a skill that goes beyond consumption, enabling users to actively dissect and understand the content they encounter, protecting themselves against the tide of misinformation.

Linking Google's Digital Well-Being initiative to the broader context of educational empowerment in the Digital Age, we see a comprehensive approach towards fostering digital literacy and healthy online habits.

Google's efforts extend beyond providing tools for managing screen time and distractions. They have also launched a series of Digital Wellbeing videos as part of Google's Digital Workshop. These videos, created in collaboration with psychologists, anthropologists, and mindfulness experts, encourage users to reflect on their technology use and suggest ways to find a balanced digital life.

These educational materials cover a wide range of topics, from managing children's technology use to effective mobile phone usage. The aim is to make these resources available in more than 30 languages across 64 countries, reflecting Google's commitment to global digital literacy and well-being. By equipping users with the knowledge to navigate the digital landscape wisely, Google is contributing to a more informed and conscious digital citizenry.

While the initiatives highlighted showcase a promising trajectory, there's still extensive ground to cover. It's essential that efforts in this sphere continually evolve to match the pace of technological advancement. Collaboration across industries, government bodies, and educational institutions will be vital in creating a comprehensive, holistic approach to ethical digital empowerment.

The next generation, raised alongside these educational programs, has the chance to inherit a digital landscape that aligns with ethical principles and prioritizes user well-being. By instilling concepts of digital literacy, critical thinking, and responsible data handling at a young age, we sow the seeds for a future where technology truly serves and enhances humanity.

The future we envision is one where algorithms are not merely opaque forces shaping our digital experiences, but transparent tools understood and harnessed by an informed populace. It's a future where technology amplifies human potential rather than diminishes it, contributing to a society anchored in individual well-being, critical thought, and informed decision-making. The initiatives we've explored are promising steps on this path. May their spirit of ethical development and user empowerment continue to spread and strengthen, guiding us towards a Digital Age that truly serves us all.

We are at a crossroads where technology's role in our lives can either amplify our human potential or complicate our pursuit of a fulfilled and ethical existence. Chapter 5 "Human Needs 2.0: A Guide to the ALIVE Framework" will guide us through this delicate balance, encouraging a mindful approach to integrating technology—a tool that should enhance, not dictate, the quality of our lives and our interactions with the world around us. By fostering a deeper understanding and critical approach, we can ensure that technology remains a servant to human progress, not the master of our destinies.

CHAPTER 4 TAKEAWAYS

Our digital lives have become incredibly distracting. Algorithms designed to keep us hooked contribute to shorter attention spans, anxiety, and overwhelm. Even the tech creators who build these platforms understand the dangers, but their focus remains on profit. We face a choice: accept this or take action. Here's how we can act:

Creator Responsibility

Ethical Algorithms: platforms must shift from focusing on user engagement to promoting our mental well-being. Algorithms should be designed to educate, inform, and support rather than simply captivate us.

User Empowerment

Befriending the Algorithm: we need to understand how algorithms function to shape our online experiences. By actively curating content and setting limits, we can train algorithms to better reflect our interests.

Educational Initiatives: learning about algorithms and teaching critical thinking skills are crucial.

This isn't just about individual awareness. We need:

○ *Transparency: platforms must be clear about how our data is used and how algorithms work.*
○ *User Feedback*: we should actively help shape platform development through feedback mechanisms.

Collective Action: online communities can help us share strategies and work together to demand ethical design and usage practices.

By combining creator responsibility and user empowerment, we can build a digital landscape that respects mental health, promotes growth, and serves the next generation's needs.

DISCOVERING AND DEFINING SELF IN THE SCREEN AGE

PART 2

In Part 2, we embark on a transitional phase of our journey, illuminating the capabilities of both technology and humanity. This section delves into how technological advancements are not just expanding what tools can do, but also enhancing human potential. Here, we showcase a range of technological applications and their transformative effects on human life. Through this exploration, we prepare readers to not only understand but fully engage with the complex concepts awaiting in the last part of the book. Through this exploration, we equip readers with the insights necessary to recognize the vast possibilities where humans and technology transcend mere survival. This paves the way for reshaping our futures at the frontier of endless possibilities in previously unimaginable ways and understanding the concept of becoming not just alive, but living indefinitely.

Chapter 5 explores how technology taps into our fundamental human needs. Drawing on theories like Maslow's hierarchy of needs and the ALIVE framework, we'll examine why technology feels so compelling. While it changes how we meet our needs, the underlying drives remain timeless. The challenge lies in using technology without becoming dependent on it for instant gratification, deep learning, validation, or self-esteem. This chapter is about understanding the interplay, not judging technology as inherently good or bad.

Chapter 6 examines how the Digital Age empowers us to redefine success. With boundless options, we're driven by individual values and dreams rather than solely traditional career paths. This chapter explores how the drive and tech skills of younger generations can blend with the experience of older ones in a future where success is about meaningful contribution and a blend of traditional and innovative approaches.

Chapter 7 delves into the multi-faceted nature of intelligence. It challenges the sole focus on IQ, emphasizing the importance of emotional intelligence (EQ) and spiritual intelligence (SQ). To cultivate a well-rounded mind, we can enhance our IQ through interactive learning and immersive experiences. EQ can be developed with apps designed to improve communication and conflict resolution skills. Mindfulness tools and exploring diverse philosophies can nurture our SQ. This chapter underscores that technology isn't just a distraction—it can be a powerful tool for enhancing all aspects of intelligence.

Chapter 8 looks to a future where technology could directly enhance our brains. Imagine a world with augmented empathy and compassion. We'll discuss the technical advances that make this possible and the profound ethical questions they raise. We'll examine potential impacts on work, communication, and equality, as well as the incredible possibilities for those with disabilities. Alongside the excitement, this chapter emphasizes the need for understanding brain science, nanotechnology, and advanced computing systems.

HUMAN NEEDS 2.0: A GUIDE TO THE ALIVE FRAMEWORK

Our technology, our machines, is part of our humanity. We created them to extend ourselves, and that is what is unique about human beings.

—Ray Kurzweil

D o you remember when the internet first started to become a part of our everyday lives? Imagine a family computer running Windows 98, with its iconic island wallpaper and the unmistakable sound of dial-up internet ready to connect us to the world.

I was an 11-year-old, eyes filled with curiosity, when my father brought home a CD-ROM, its surface shining in our living room light. The CD was labeled "Encarta." Filled with eagerness and curiosity, I inserted it into our desktop, and suddenly, I found myself in a limitless universe of knowledge that seemed both vast and infinitely accessible.

Encarta wasn't just an encyclopedia; it was my weekend adventure, my ticket to galaxies far beyond my backyard. It was a gateway to exploration for a kid who had always found traditional books a bit tedious. Astronomy became more than a subject—it became my passion. Here I was, a kid who would do anything to avoid reading a book, now printing out pages upon pages about stars, planets, and galaxies. This digital resource transformed me from a reluctant reader into an eager learner, and even further, into a passionate researcher and content creator, especially in the realm of astronomy. This tool represented not just a leap forward in accessing information, but a profound transformation in the very nature of learning itself, embodying the seamless integration of technology with daily life, turning curiosity-driven exploration into a tangible, interactive experience.

Then, there was MSN Messenger. It felt like suddenly being granted the power to teleport, connecting with friends, classmates, and even mysterious neighbors from down the street. The boundaries of our little worlds were suddenly stretched wide open. My sister, the digital pirate she was, managed to download thousands of mp4 audios using eMule, a free file-sharing app that was like a treasure chest of entertainment.

Remember the excitement of watching a download bar slowly fill up? Or the joy when the printer finally worked? And how about the buzz from our first mobile phones? Getting texts or calls, taking our first grainy photos. Those days were full of fun, curiosity, and excitement, but mainly, they were about change and new discoveries.

You might ask, "Why are we embarking on this journey into the past?" It's not just for the sake of nostalgia, it's about understanding the profound impact of technology on our lives. It wasn't merely for entertainment or convenience that we turned to these digital tools. They fulfilled deeper needs—connecting us, expanding our knowledge, and offering new ways to express ourselves.

But why has technology become such a big part of our lives? Was it all for fun, or was there something deeper we were reaching for? How these screens and gadgets moved from being interesting toys to essentials makes us rethink our first impressions of tech.

I used to think that technology was made to distract us, a tool created by society only to make more money. But I rarely considered: what if technology was also made to help us? What if we were the ones who really pushed its development?

To get into these questions, I ran a simple survey to see what people of different ages think. The early results showed that the majority believe the internet was born from both human needs and desires, as well as the ambitions of certain groups or companies. Additionally, many people shared a positive view: the internet and social media have been very important for both learning new things and improving our lives. They've helped fix a lot of our old misunderstandings about different topics. This shows us how powerful these tools are in giving us better information and helping us see the world more clearly.

These insights made me reconsider technology all over again, from the ground up. I started to look closely at our simple, basic needs as humans and how technology has changed them over time, focusing on exploring the essential needs of humans and observing how they've changed through history with the development of technology.

WHERE DID WE BEGIN?

Every move we make, every choice we endorse, is rooted in a purpose, a driving need. Nothing is just random. To truly understand this, we need to tap into the wisdom of scientists and philosophers who've tried to decode our human desires and motivations over centuries. It's fascinating to see how our needs have evolved with time. This isn't about deciding if technology is good or bad, but more about understanding the real minds behind its creation. We must ask: was it our own inner calling or an external force that crafted this tech-driven world?

This chapter delves deeper than a mere historical recount. It reveals a critical truth: many believe that technology changes our fundamental needs, creating superfluous ones. We frequently misunderstand, thinking technology has replaced essential needs or created new supposed essential needs. But in reality, technology has simply exposed needs that were always there, just not yet visible. My aim is to demonstrate that our interaction with technology is primarily about discovery, not dependency. It's about uncovering hidden needs and envisioning new possibilities for life and opportunities. This journey with technology is not just about what we need; it's about exploring the unknown and revealing the deeper aspects of our existence.

Throughout history, many have explored the complex landscape of the human spirit and needs. American psychologist Abraham Maslow's hierarchy of needs is well known, but there are also theories like Harvard Business School professors Paul Lawrence and Nitin Nohria's Four-Drive Theory and American psychologist David McClelland's Theory of Needs that offer insight. Inspired by these insights, I developed the ALIVE framework to shed light on human motivations and how they evolve, especially with the advent of digital technology. ALIVE breaks down into: A for "acquisition," focusing on our drive to gather resources; L for "learning," which covers our pursuit of knowledge; I for "incentive," relating to our motivation; V for "validation," about seeking acknowledgement from others; and E for "esteem," which involves our need for self-respect and recognition. This framework aims to elucidate each of these primal needs while shedding light on the significant role of technology in unveiling new opportunities, perspectives, and forms of life.

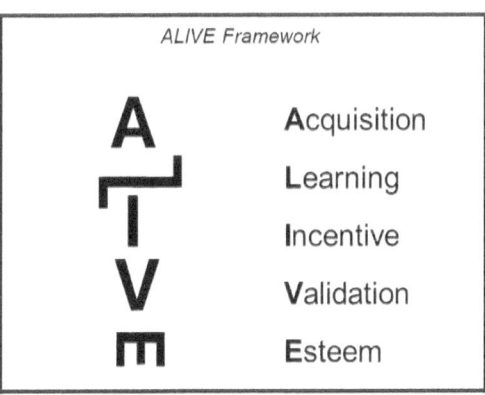

ALIVE Framework

A — Acquisition
I — Learning
V — Incentive
V — Validation
E — Esteem

ACQUISITION: HAVING IT VS. HAVING IT NOW

Throughout history, humankind has always been driven to acquire—a primal instinct, a deep-rooted urge to possess an asset. From the times when early people hunted for food to survive, to kingdoms growing bigger, to people today buying things to show off, our stories have always been about getting and owning things. But as the pages of history turn, and time evolves, so does our urgency for acquisition. Back then, we waited patiently. Now, we want things IMMEDIATELY.

In modern societies, the timeline of desire has dramatically shifted. Historically, patience was a virtue born of necessity; our ancestors had no choice but to wait for the seasons to change for harvests or endure long periods before receiving goods from distant lands. Today, however, we live in an age characterized by an expectation of immediacy. The underlying question is: What has driven this shift towards impatience?

This transformation can be linked to technological advancements and the rise of a convenience culture. The advent of the internet, fast shipping, and instant communication has redefined our expectations. Where once the delay was anticipated and accepted, now any waiting is often seen as a pointless delay. This impatience isn't just a cultural shift; it's deeply rooted in the evolution of our societal structures and technological capabilities. We've transitioned from a world where time moved slowly, dictated by scarcity—resources were limited and waiting for necessities was often long and tedious, reflecting the "born dead" concept of enduring boredom—to a fast-paced era shaped by abundance, where technology provides near-instant access to information, goods, and services, enabling us to live fully and seek new experiences rapidly, embodying a state of being more "alive."

Companies today build products that respond quickly because they know we don't like to wait. This isn't just about making things more accessible or easier to use; it's about fitting into our fast-paced lives. The success of grocery and food delivery services, sometimes delivering to us in under an hour, exemplifies a world where what we want is just a tap away.

Then there's Amazon, a giant that has redefined what fast means. With services like Prime, it promises deliveries so quick it almost feels like the moment you think of something, it's already on its way.

But why this shift towards wanting everything now? Because every second that passes reminds us that life is short. We want to make the most of every moment, which makes us crave instant results. Also, this push for immediacy has become intertwined with our pursuit of happiness. The faster we get what we desire, the more we believe it contributes to our joy. Our constant connection to the digital world shows us all we could have, making us want things now more than ever.

Forward Reflections: Preserving Value in the Age of Speed

In our race to get everything instantly, we must pause and reflect: by having everything at our fingertips, do we unintentionally diminish its value? Or are we simply enjoying the benefits of both saved time and the acquired object? Moreover, as we transition from tangible items to digital assets, do they hold the same sentimental value? Or do digital treasures, with their permanence and resistance to time's decay, offer a different, perhaps more enduring, kind of value?

The age of immediacy, for all its allure, is a double-edged sword. It grants us unparalleled access and speed yet poses challenges that resonate at an existential level. As we move forward, the challenge is twofold:

- To harness the power of technology without becoming slaves to the instant
- To ensure that our acquisitions, swift as they may be, still hold meaning and value

Time, as they say, waits for no one. But perhaps, in our quest for acquisition in the Digital Age, it's essential for us to occasionally pause, reflect, and ask: in our bid to have it all now, what is it that we're truly seeking?

LEARNING: SEEKING THE TRUTH

From our earliest days, curiosity has always been a driving force for humans. The push to understand our world, solve its puzzles, and uncover truths has always been at the core of being human. Our quest for knowledge has taken many forms. Early humans shared knowledge through oral stories around fires, which was our first way of making sense of the world and passing wisdom to others.

Historically, learning was a ritual, a sacred journey where the seeker would set out, often for their whole lifetime, in search of truth. Sacred texts, scriptures, and religious discourses were among the treasured routes to this wisdom. Our ancestors sought answers to life's biggest mysteries, often turning to religion and philosophy to understand the world's intricate design. They yearned to comprehend their place in this vast universe and the very purpose of existence.

From our earliest thoughts, we realized two important things. First, our deep need to understand and find the truth is as basic as our need for food and a place to live. Second, the journey to uncover these truths is complicated. It's like navigating a maze that requires patience, hard work, and sometimes, a whole lifetime to explore.

This quest for knowledge and truth is part of what makes us human. It drives us to ask big questions about our world and ourselves, pushing us to look beyond the surface. For millennia, we've grappled with profound mysteries such as the origin of the universe—where did everything come from, how did it begin, and will it ever end? We ponder the nature of consciousness, questioning what it is and whether it's unique to humans or shared with other animals. We explore the possibility of extraterrestrial life, wondering whether we are alone in the universe or if there are other life forms out there. But finding answers isn't straightforward. It's a process filled with challenges and obstacles, much like the way inventors and scientists work through problems, experimenting and learning as they go. Our current understanding of science is not final and can evolve with time and technological advancements.

Early humans relied on oral traditions to pass down knowledge from generation to generation. Stories, songs, and teachings were shared around campfires and in tribal gatherings. However, this method had its limitations: information could be easily lost or distorted over time, and access was confined to those within a specific community.

A significant breakthrough occurred with the development of writing. This innovation allowed for the creation of permanent records, such as scrolls and eventually books. Written knowledge could now be preserved for longer periods and shared with a wider audience. However, it's important to acknowledge that literacy was initially a privilege of the few—often limited to elites or religious scholars. Nevertheless, the advent of writing and libraries marked a significant leap forward in the preservation and dissemination of knowledge across generations.

As we've progressed, the essence of our learning has taken on a new dimension. It's no longer about simply acquiring knowledge; it's about sifting through the sea of information to unlock new realities and expand our understanding of the world. This journey for truth is not just a casual endeavor; it's become a critical mission in our lives. With the Digital Age flooding us with endless streams of content, discerning what is true from what is false has never been more challenging—or more important.

Our quest for knowledge drives us to seek innovative and efficient ways to learn, ways that not only engage us but also lead us directly to the heart of truth. This pursuit is deeply personal yet universally shared, reflecting our collective yearning to understand our world and our place within it truly. As we navigate through the complexities of modern information, our goal remains steadfast: to peel away layers of misinformation and reach the core of genuine knowledge. In this relentless pursuit, we're not just learners; we're truth-seekers, armed with curiosity and empowered by technology to chase after the real insights that shape our understanding of the world.

Today, we are overwhelmed with information. A question arises in the mind, and within seconds, answers from all corners of the globe are available. While this is a testament to human progress, it presents a poignant dichotomy. In our haste to understand everything instantly, are we missing out on the profound depths of wisdom that only come with time and reflection? Does turning learning into a game dilute its essence? Or does it simply make the process more engaging, ensuring consistent involvement? With knowledge at our fingertips, do we truly appreciate its worth? Are we driven to explore new truths and delve into the unknown? Or do we simply transmit existing knowledge between generations? Or do we actively challenge and expand upon it?

Forward Reflections: Focusing on the Unknown

Time might be racing ahead, but perhaps, in our pursuit of knowledge in this accelerated world, there's a need for deliberate pause, a step back to ponder what truly matters. For decades, our educational systems have operated on redundancy, often imposing massive learning without genuine purpose. Generations have been fed with repeated knowledge, creating a cycle that, while safe, can be limited. We've been learning what's known, following familiar paths, often ignoring the enigmatic, the unknown, the areas yet to be explored.

While advancements in technology and science have been phenomenal, vast mysteries remain. For example, we still grapple with understanding dark matter and dark energy, which constitute most of the universe but elude our current knowledge.

This is precisely why education shouldn't solely focus on established facts. It should ignite a passion for the unknown, nurturing a spirit of inquiry in students. Imagine if, throughout their academic journey, students were encouraged to delve into the enigmatic corners of science, much like researchers do. This wouldn't require waiting until advanced degrees; the seeds of curiosity and independent exploration can be planted from the very beginning.

Now, more than ever, as seekers of truth, our focus should pivot to those unexplored areas. We stand at a precipice of unparalleled potential, with AI and cutting-edge tools at our disposal, capable of dissecting complex patterns, predicting outcomes, and delivering insights that the human mind might overlook. The promise they hold is not just of speed but depth, allowing us to dive into realms previously hard to understand.

To truly progress, we need to cultivate a culture of curious inquiry in our society, one that doesn't just accept the known but seeks to question it. A culture that prioritizes discovering over simply knowing. For in this quest, in the brave pursuit of what lies beyond our current understanding, we might just uncover truths that propel humanity forward in ways we've only dreamed of. Learning isn't just about knowing; it's about exploring the new. Technology shouldn't hold us back, but guide us forward.

INCENTIVE: WHAT KEEPS US GOING AFTER SUCCESS

Since the beginning of human history, our drive to thrive has shaped our actions. Our early ancestors traded goods and sought fertile lands, but today, the quest for financial wealth dominates. The incentive to earn, to accumulate wealth, is now more than just a means for survival; it has become a marker of success, a ticket to a higher social standing, and a tool for self-validation.

Historically, wealth was measured in tangible assets: livestock, land, or the size of one's clan, directly linking possessions to power and influence. Fast forward a few hundred years, and the scenario began to shift.

With the dawn of democracy, industrialization and urbanization, earnings weren't just for survival; they became measures of success. The better car, the bigger house, the fatter bank account—all became symbols of a person having "made it." It's important to acknowledge that this is a simplified picture. The rise of consumerism, the growing influence of advertising, and cultural shifts have all played significant roles in shaping our current association of wealth with success.

Why this inexorable pull towards accumulating more money and resources? Because currency, in its various forms, provided people with choice, freedom, and power. In a world governed by transactional dynamics, those with more resources wielded more influence.

Yet, with the emergence of the Digital Age, our perceptions of wealth and incentives have shifted once again. Money, while still pivotal, is now complemented by digital assets, online influence, and virtual currencies. Cryptocurrencies, social media influence, online reputations—these have added nuanced layers to our understanding of prosperity. The lines between tangible and intangible incentives are blurring. Nonetheless, the underlying motivation persists: the world continues to chase after more—more acknowledgement, not merely for the sake of amassing wealth, but for the experiences, authority, and recognition it can unlock.

Forward Reflections: New Rich in the Digital Era

Incentive, at its core, drives the human desire for social recognition and value. Historically, wealth served as the primary metric for such status. Technology undoubtedly disrupts this traditional paradigm by offering new pathways to success and recognition. Digital platforms empower individuals with talent and initiative to build careers and potentially earn significant incomes, challenging the old adage "the rich get richer." Social media influencers, YouTubers, and online entrepreneurs can rise to prominence based on their skills and creativity, not just inherited wealth.

However, the full potential of these opportunities is not yet clear to the economically disadvantaged due to persistent disparities. Access to reliable internet, quality education, and the skills necessary to thrive in the digital age remain unevenly distributed. Looking ahead to the future, I believe that these disparities will diminish radically. Consider what tools like Open AI have already done for developers without formal coding education—I know many such people. Similarly, Open Data has created multiple opportunities for entrepreneurs. Just look at the impact in 2024. So, what about in the next 70 to 100 years?

Before the digital revolution, societal norms and systems often favored those who were already in positions of wealth and power. Birthright, lineage, and access to traditional education often dictated one's trajectory. But today, technology levels the playing field. The internet doesn't care about your family name, where you were born, or the depth of your pockets. It respects skill, innovation, and genuine talent. Whether it's a self-taught coder building the next big software or a gifted artist showcasing their work on Instagram, technology has amplified the voice of the truly talented, allowing them to rise based on merit, not just legacy.

This shift is not just commendable, but also deeply necessary. For a society to truly progress, it must recognize and reward genuine talent, irrespective of its origin. Technology, in this sense, has made the world fairer. Now, a person's worth isn't just tied to their lineage or their bank balance but to their ideas, their drive, and their ability to bring about change.

Yet, as we celebrate this evolution, we must also tread with caution. While technology offers unprecedented opportunities, it also comes with its set of challenges. The choice is ours: it's on us to utilize these digital tools responsibly, ensuring that while we chase incentives, we don't lose sight of values like integrity, empathy, and societal welfare.

In our relentless pursuit of more, it's essential to remember that the ultimate incentive isn't just wealth or recognition, but a life lived with purpose, meaning, and genuine connection. The Digital Age, with all its potential, provides us with the tools to achieve this—but it's up to us to use them wisely.

At the end, what is the ultimate incentive? Wealth may provide experiences, but can we find deeper meaning in contribution? Technology gives us the tools—the wisdom of their use is up to us.

VALIDATION: THE UNYIELDING QUEST FOR SOCIAL ACCEPTANCE

Our human journey transcends the pursuit of material possessions. We crave validation—acknowledgement, smiles, social media "likes"—because they signify acceptance. We long to belong, to be seen, and to matter. But why is this need so fundamental?

Historically, community wasn't just social, it was essential for survival. Exclusion from a tribe could even mean death. This hardwired the need for validation, linking it to security and belonging. It's not merely ego; it echoes a primal instinct for safety within a group.

With the rise of civilizations, communities, and societal structures, the layers of validation became intricate. It wasn't just about being part of a tribe now; it was about one's standing within that tribe. The titles, the acknowledgements, the positions of power—all became indicators of one's worth.

Flash forward to our modern Digital Age, and the need for validation has increased exponentially. Social media platforms, which many initially adopted for connectivity, have unknowingly become arenas for seeking validation. Every post, every tweet, every photo is, in essence, a shout into the void saying, "See me, hear me, validate me." It's not merely about sharing; it's about the reactions that follow. We equate "likes," shares, and comments with validation, acceptance, and occasionally, our self-worth.

Yet, the Digital Age has also democratized validation to some extent. Before, societal hierarchies and established norms often determined who received validation. Now, with the internet, a young artist from a remote village can receive appreciation from someone on the other side of the globe. The barriers have crumbled, giving rise to a more inclusive form of validation, but this change also brings its own set of challenges.

Herein lies the heart of the matter: does this digital applause equate to genuine validation? Would we be as enthusiastic about sharing our lives on platforms like Facebook or Instagram if "likes" or reactions were removed? Probably not. We're no longer just seeking validation; we're addicted to its digital metric. It's quantified validation.

This raises important questions: is there a danger in chasing the numbers, rather than focusing on the quality of our work or connections? How is the need for digital validation shaping our online behavior? Does it lead to more authentic self-expression or curated performances? Are social media companies ethically responsible for how their platforms influence our self-worth?

Forward Reflections: Toward Authenticity

As the digital curtain unfolds, our pursuit of validation increasingly becomes a quest for unattainable perfection. But whose standard of perfection are we chasing? Today, more than ever, there's a tangible pressure to curate our lives to fit standards fueled by societal perceptions and pressures, amplified by social media. We aren't just sharing moments; we're presenting meticulously edited highlights, seeking applause for our "perfect" lives.

Furthermore, this continuous exposure to everyone's "best moments" can lead to relentless self-comparison. The digital era gives us a wider lens, but it also casts long shadows of doubt, making us question our achievements, our lifestyles, and even our self-worth. With everyone's life seemingly an open book, we've started to have an enhanced perspective, or rather scrutiny, of ourselves. This newfound introspection, driven by the Digital Age, means we're constantly re-evaluating our place in this vast digital social hierarchy.

For authentic validation in the Digital Age, it's crucial to address these challenges:

- *Reject the illusion.* Avoid equating digital perfection with real-world self-worth. The "perfect" moments others showcase are but a fraction of their lives, as are ours.
- *Embrace the authentic.* Embrace authenticity over curated perfection. It's vital to remember that true validation stems from being genuine rather than fitting an image.
- *Channel introspection positively*: Leverage the introspection that the Digital Age brings positively. Instead of being hypercritical, we should use this self-awareness for growth, understanding, and self-improvement.

In sum, as we sail through the digital seas in search of validation, it's essential to keep our compass pointed towards authenticity. In a world that often blurs the lines between the real and the virtual, the true north lies in understanding and valuing ourselves, beyond "likes" and beyond digital applause.

ESTEEM: CRAFTING IDENTITY IN A DIGITIZED WORLD

In every individual's heart lies a quest for self-worth. Esteem is not just self-fulfillment, but it's intertwined with the essence of who we are—our identity. Throughout history, brave warriors were recognized for their courage, scholars for their insights, and artists for their unique perspectives and creativity. Their societal recognition, while augmenting their personal esteem, was also a testament to their unique identity. This recognition was not merely about societal titles but an affirmation that whispered, "I have value, I am seen, I matter."

Today, social media is a new arena for seeking validation. The "like" button becomes a metric of self-worth for many. This highlights a complex dance between external approval and inner esteem. While linked, they serve different needs. Validation craves outward approval. Esteem is deeply personal, tied to our core identity and essential for well-being.

Our digital interactions, in many ways, serve as mirrors, reflecting our need for acknowledgement and simultaneously shaping our sense of self-worth. Every share, comment, and digital interaction can either fortify or fracture our esteem. But herein lies a potent question: are these digital platforms truly authentic mirrors of our identity, or are they merely curated reflections designed for societal approval? The development of authentic self-esteem and a healthy sense of self has always been a vitally important part of growing up, and in an age where judgments are swift and ubiquitous, this becomes even more crucial.

In this age, as our digital personas receive feedback, it's not merely our online self that's affected. The ripples touch our core, influencing our self-perception and esteem. However, it's also worth noting the risk of conflating digital validation with genuine self-worth. There's a delicate balance to maintain.

Forward Reflections: The Limits of Algorithms, the Power of Self

In the wise words of Albert Einstein, "Everybody is a genius. But if you judge a fish by its ability to climb a tree, it will live its whole life believing that it is stupid." The age of algorithms, while brimming with endless potential, bears a caveat: they generalize, categorize, and sometimes, oversimplify. We live in an era where data points seek to define us, where algorithms attempt to pigeonhole our vast, intricate personalities into digestible bytes.

Algorithms can be blind to our unique potential. A few curated posts might lead a recommendation system to misunderstand our interests or skills completely. If we let these algorithms define us, we risk limiting our opportunities and growth.

As we navigate the delicate balance between external validation and internal esteem in this Digital Age, introspection becomes our beacon. With so many platforms at our fingertips painting myriad digital personas, it's pivotal to introspect on the essence behind our online interactions. Is it the desire for digital applause we respond to or the resonance of genuine connection? Do we navigate the digital realms chasing the transient glow of validation, or are we laying bricks of esteem, steady and resilient?

Our true challenge isn't merely navigating the digital realm, but doing so while retaining the authenticity of our identity. It's about recognizing that while algorithms and data points can offer insights, they cannot capture the entirety of our being. True esteem isn't constructed from digital titles. It comes from an authentic core, nurtured by genuine experiences, enriched by self-awareness, and untouched by the fickleness of online validations.

In a world increasingly driven by quantifiable metrics and algorithmic predictions, perhaps our quest is to seek that invaluable qualitative essence—our authentic self. In this journey, while algorithms can guide, only introspection can enlighten.

THE ESSENCE OF ALIVE IN THE DIGITAL ERA

Our journey through the ALIVE framework has led us down paths of introspection, societal analysis, and forward-looking speculation, revealing that our human needs, while age-old, are constantly evolving in meaning and representation.

ALIVE Framework: Recommendations for a Balanced Tech-Powered Future		
	From...	**To...**
Acquisition ➡	Material Possessions	Meaningful Experiences
Learning ➡	Established Facts	Unexplored Areas
Incentive ➡	Financial Gain	Passionate Purpose
Validation ➡	Societal Approval	Authentic Self-Worth
Esteem ➡	Prestige and Titles	Inner Fulfillment

Acquisition has always been about obtaining what we need and desire. But in our rapid-paced society, it's no longer just about having, but having now. This urgency has given a new dimension to the concept of value. Value isn't just inherent in objects or experiences; it's also defined by the time and effort we save in acquiring them.

When we think about learning, we don't just seek knowledge but the truth. We aim to understand the very fabric of existence, the mysteries that surround us, and the deeper meanings of life. It's not the quantity of knowledge, but the quality of understanding that matters.

Incentive, driven by our quest for rewards, is no longer just about personal gains but ensuring everyone gets their rightful share. It underscores fairness in a world that's shifting from material wealth to ethical richness.

In our Digital Age, validation is about connecting, about reaching out and feeling the pulse of the world. It's about understanding others and being understood, fostering empathy in a world of "likes" and "shares."

Lastly, esteem speaks to our core, our very identity. In an era where algorithms often dictate preferences, authenticity becomes our compass in the digital sea. It means holding true to ourselves amidst the endless distractions.

In our pursuit of the digital, of the instantaneous, of the algorithmic, we mustn't lose sight of what truly matters: the inherent value of experiences, the truth in knowledge, fairness in our incentives, empathy in our validations, and the authenticity of our self-worth.

Let's strive not just to be digitally ALIVE but to truly live in every sense of the word. For in understanding and balancing these dimensions, we do more than merely exist—we thrive, we "die alive."

REFLECTION SPACE: YOUR DIGITAL SELF IN THE TAPESTRY OF ALIVE

Acquisition & Value

- Ponder moments when technology played a pivotal role in acquiring something significant. How different would it have been in a world less connected?
- With the ease technology offers, are there instances where you intentionally delay gratification? Why might that be?

Learning & Truth

- Reflect on how technology has ushered you into realms you never imagined. Are there topics or interests you've discovered solely because of the digital world?
- Given the vastness of knowledge, which areas do you feel are yet undiscovered or understood? How might technological advancements, particularly AI, be utilized to explore these areas further?

Incentive & Fairness

- Recall instances where technology has given you or someone you know an advantage. Perhaps a chance that wouldn't have existed otherwise.
- In what ways do you feel technology has democratized opportunities? Conversely, where might it be perpetuating disparities?

Validation & Empathy

- Delve into moments of genuine connection in the digital realm. When and how have online interactions deeply resonated with you?
- Amidst "likes," comments, and shares, how do you discern between see king external validation and maintaining genuine connections?

Esteem & Authenticity

- Think about how your digital interactions might have shaped your self-perception. Have certain apps or platforms specifically influenced your self-esteem?
- Reflect on the personas you present online and offline. Are they in sync, or are there disparities?

In today's interconnected era, what aspects of your life do you feel would be most impacted without technology? How do you imagine your daily routine, work, social interactions, and hobbies would transform in a tech-devoid world?

As you reflect on these ideas, be cognizant of the ALIVE framework's essence in your life. Recognize how each facet interacts with technology, shaping your perceptions, behaviors, and aspirations.

And so we conclude our exploration of the ALIVE framework in this chapter, revealing how our fundamental needs—from acquisition to esteem—have remained constant throughout history. The crucial takeaway? Technology doesn't create entirely new needs; it shapes how we fulfill them. These foundational insights set the stage for Chapter 6, where we delve into the practical outcomes of these shifts, particularly among the younger generations who navigate this digital landscape as natives.

CHAPTER 5 TAKEAWAYS

Technology shapes our lives, but it's important to remember that it's a tool, not our master. Our fundamental human needs—to acquire, learn, seek validation, etc.—are timeless, but how we fulfill them has changed. Chapter 5 explored this delicate balance through the ALIVE framework: acquisition, learning, incentive, validation, and esteem.

Technology can enhance or complicate fulfilling our core needs—the choice is ours.

Questioning the instant gratification culture can help us preserve meaning in our lives.

When using technology, focus on depth of understanding, not just accumulation of information.

May we strive for a world where technology fosters fairness for all.

While navigating digital spaces, it's critical to prioritize authenticity and true connections.

Remember, self-worth is built from the inside out, not by algorithms.

By understanding the interplay between our needs and technology (the ALIVE framework), we can make choices that lead to genuine fulfillment, not just digital trophies.

ECHOES OF GENERATIONS: FROM DIGITAL DIVIDE TO DIGITAL HARMONY

The test of our progress is not whether we add more to the abundance of those who have much, it is whether we provide enough for those who have little.

—Franklin D. Roosevelt

A t 24, embarking on my career, I found myself in a landscape rich with opportunities but also riddled with uncertainties. I realized when I was working as a consultant that many people at work were doing things in parallel. I remember one colleague who was a chef and gaining popularity as an influencer on Instagram, making money from it alongside his day job. Another was a comedian while also working as an auditor in a big firm. Then there was a consultant just two years older than me who shared his feelings of dissatisfaction with his job. He didn't see the value in what he was doing and felt a deeper calling for something more meaningful. Not only was he freelancing as a consultant, which provided a steady income, but he was also pursuing his passion for travel and exploration.

Years later, I became curious about many of these colleagues. It seemed that many in Generation Y were reassessing their careers, eager to explore new avenues that aligned more closely with their passions and interests. This shift, facilitated largely by the digital tools and platforms at our disposal, was reshaping our professional landscape. It's a testament to the transformative power of technology in our careers and lives. Seeing joy in living a life true to our desires was inspiring.

The unprecedented pace of technological change has created distinct generational divides, shaping how individuals relate to work, life, and society. My generation, Generation Y, born into the Digital Age, has been uniquely positioned to redefine success. With the world at our fingertips, we have the tools and the reach to pursue diverse and unconventional career paths. However, this abundance of choice also brings the challenge of finding our place in a rapidly changing landscape.

While this fluidity and adaptability come naturally to many of our generation, these traits contrast sharply with the approaches favored by older generations. This leads to a significant disconnect and potential conflicts in workplaces and broader society.

In this curious dance between generations, the steps are often misaligned, leading to stumbles and missteps rather than a harmonious performance. These conflicts reveal a profound disconnect in values, expectations, and modes of operation.

While older generations cling to a methodical, time-tested approach, the younger seek fluidity, adaptability, and a more humane integration of work and life. It's not a matter of mere preference; it's a clash of philosophies, each deeply rooted and fiercely defended.

What are the defining traits of this new generation? How has technology changed the mindsets and behaviors of these generations? How will this lead to societal conflicts or heightened anxiety? Despite these challenges, how can we redefine success and instill a sense of hope for the next generations?

The answers may not come easily, but the questions themselves are a crucial starting point. In the exploration of these generational divides, we may discover not only a path forward but a richer, more nuanced understanding of who we are and who we can become.

FROM GEN "WHY" TO GEN "ZEN"

The rapid pace of technological change has created a generational divide, shaping how we approach work, life, and our place within society. We are the "whY" Generation (as I like to call us), always questioning the old norms and navigating a plethora of possibilities, trying to craft our own narratives of success and satisfaction. Gen Y, born between 1981 and 1996, represents not just a demographic but the driving forces shaping a new era. They came of age amidst a technological revolution; the digital landscape is not merely a backdrop but an integral part of their cognitive and social fabric. For Gen Y, the internet has transcended its role as a tool, becoming a catalyst for redefining what it means to be connected, informed, and engaged. But this is not without its challenges; increased stress and anxiety are commonplace as generational conflicts arise. The rapid pace of technological development hasn't been mirrored in people's mindsets, creating significant friction within society. Older

generations often struggle to accept change, criticizing younger ones—
even those of Gen Y, who seem remarkably adaptable—for their distinct
approaches.

As we shift our focus to Generation Z, or as I like to call them, the
"Zen" Generation, we encounter a distinct set of traits and attitudes
towards work and life. Gen Z takes digital immersion even further.
As the first generation to grow up entirely in the age of the internet,
Generation Z (born post-1996) isn't merely adapting to the digital
world—they are redefining it. Their relationship with technology goes
beyond proficiency; it's an intrinsic part of their identity, profoundly
influencing interactions, aspirations, and perspectives. Gen Z steps
into the workforce with a confidence that borders on audacity. Their
deep-seated comfort with technology, born from a lifetime of digital
immersion, gives them a unique edge in a tech-centric world. They
exhibit a "know-it-all" attitude, often surprising older colleagues with
their readiness to not just learn but also to teach.

This constant exposure to technology has instilled in them a belief
that anything is possible. Challenges are seen not as roadblocks but
as opportunities to innovate. Their approach to work is marked by a
distinctive "can-do" attitude, where changing jobs or career paths is not
daunting but an exciting opportunity for growth and exploration. They
possess an inherent optimism about their abilities to make a positive
impact in their chosen fields.

However, this unwavering confidence can sometimes be perceived as
overconfidence or a lack of respect for experience. Gen Z's reliance on
technology and their digital-first mindset also brings about a unique
set of challenges in the workplace. They tend to favor quick, efficient
solutions, which can sometimes overlook the importance of deep,
analytical thinking and face-to-face interactions.

Studies have shown that Gen Z values individual expression, flexibility,
and the opportunity to pursue work that is aligned with their personal
values and passions.[1] Research by McKinsey & Company found that

nearly half (45%) of Gen Z individuals express concerns about the stability of their employment.[2] To meet these expectations, employers should balance the need for flexible work options with opportunities for career development and job certainty. In an interview with the Washington Post, Julie Lee, director of technology and mental health at Harvard Alumni for Mental Health and an expert on Gen Z health and employment, summed up the work expectations of young people today: "What Gen Z wants is to do meaningful work with a sense of autonomy and flexibility, work-life balance, and work with people who work collaboratively."[3]

The same McKinsey study also shows that Gen Z is less driven by traditional measures of success, such as job titles and salaries, and places a higher emphasis on the impact they can make and the experiences they can gain. This generation is more likely to accept a job that aligns with their interests, even if it offers a lower salary. To attract and retain young workers, organizations should focus on emphasizing their mission, values, and the positive impact of their work—factors that resonate with Gen Z's desire for purpose-driven careers.

In delving into the distinct characteristics and perspectives of Generations Y and Z, I recognized that this analysis provides an insightful starting point for this book. The juxtaposition of Gen Y's adaptability to technological change and Gen Z's innate digital fluency highlights the diverse ways in which technology shapes our experiences and expectations. Their unique relationship with technology—Generation Y experiencing the digital transition and Generation Z being born into it—vividly illustrates the profound impact technology has had on our society.

This exploration serves as a foundation for understanding the positive influences of technological advancements and sets the stage for the recommendations for the future we will explore. By examining these generational shifts, we can better appreciate how technology has not only reshaped our professional and personal lives but also holds the promise of continuing to drive positive change for the next generations.

THE FUTURE SHAPERS: POTENTIAL AND PITFALLS

The current generation challenges traditional notions of success and fulfillment. They question conventional paths, prioritize well-being and social impact, and seek experiences that enrich their lives and communities. Technology has not only catalyzed these shifts but provided the current generation with the means to pursue their passions and create a world more aligned with their values.

For this generation, wellness transcends physical health, embracing an integrated approach focusing on mental, emotional, and spiritual well-being. Statistics underscore this shift: 45% prioritize a holistic approach to wellness and employee fitness.[4] Social media platforms like Instagram and dedicated wellness apps provide a wealth of information, inspiration, and support networks for holistic living.

A commitment to sustainability is evident in their consumer habits, with preference given to ethically-sourced and environmentally conscious products. A significant 72% of Millennials indicate a willingness to pay more for sustainable products. This trend underscores a broader shift where younger generations, including Gen Z, who show an even higher readiness—at 73%—are leading the charge in sustainable consumption.[5] Tools like product comparison sites and online reviews empower individuals to make informed purchasing decisions aligned with their values.

The traditional 9-to-5 career trajectory is being questioned and disrupted. A substantial 40% of this generation are reevaluating their careers, prioritizing fulfillment and purpose.[6] Freelance platforms like Upwork and Fiverr offer opportunities for flexible, skill-based work while websites like Etsy allow for the creation and sale of handcrafted goods. These online resources enable individuals to design their own professional paths and achieve a more satisfying work-life balance.

Travel isn't merely a luxury for this generation but an essential component of personal growth and global awareness. Affordable travel options through websites like Kayak or Skyscanner, digital travel communities on platforms like Reddit or Facebook Groups, and platforms like Airbnb have made experiencing the world more accessible. Technology has empowered this generation to be global citizens, fostering a desire to connect with diverse cultures and perspectives, as highlighted by the statistic that they are more likely to travel abroad than previous generations.[7]

With an intuitive command of social media, this generation wields significant influence within online spaces. Platforms like Twitter, Instagram, and TikTok enable the curation of content, amplification of voices, and mobilization for social movements. Hashtags like #BlackLivesMatter and #MeToo exemplify the power of digital activism in reshaping political discourse and driving real-world change.

This generation's approach to spirituality is fluid and individualistic. Many are disillusioned with traditional religious institutions, with 30% identifying more with spirituality than organized religion.[8] They seek meaning and connection through alternative paths, aided by online meditation apps like Headspace or Calm, spiritual communities within social media platforms, and access to personalized spiritual guidance services.

This generation stands at a crossroads, their futures shaped by the choices they make today. They embrace a world in flux, but the path forward is not guaranteed. Will they find ways to reconcile conflicting worldviews and create a more inclusive and equitable future? Or will their aspirations be undermined by the persistent challenges and generational tensions they seek to overcome?

In today's rapidly evolving workplaces, stark generational divides create a complex tapestry of perspectives and workstyles. Individuals who came of age in a pre-digital world often find themselves at odds with those who have known nothing but a tech-saturated landscape. This dynamic can lead to misunderstandings, resentment, and an underlying tension as both sides struggle to understand the other.

Consider the experienced professional, whose work ethic is grounded in the values of their generation: dedication often measured by time invested and a clear distinction between work and personal spheres. They may express their commitment with sentiments like, "I didn't get to where I am by leaving the office before 8 pm" or "You can have a work-life balance only when you retire."

On the opposing side is a younger generation empowered by technology and driven by a desire for balance, fulfillment, and social impact. They view time as a resource to be managed efficiently, not merely endured. Leaving at 5 pm isn't a sign of laziness but of utilizing technology to maximize efficiency and well-being.

This clash of perspectives highlights the central role technology now plays in shaping differing expectations. The older generation may see technology as merely a tool to augment existing processes. Conversely, the younger generation, having grown up in a digital world, views technology as intrinsic to how work gets done and how they define their value within a company. This can lead to misunderstandings and resentment when those perspectives aren't acknowledged.

The effects of these conflicts aren't confined to the office. They permeate the way we perceive success, wealth, and ambition. Research indicates that the rise of the gig economy and freelance work is driven largely by younger generations. Unlike those before them, they often don't see job security as the ultimate career goal. They are entrepreneurial, willing to take calculated risks, and comfortable with a nonlinear career path.

This generation's comfort with technology gives them a distinct advantage in a rapidly changing world. Their familiarity with new concepts often leads to a sense of self-assuredness and a strong desire for impact. This translates into valuable contributions in adapting to market shifts and bringing fresh perspectives to the workplace.

The impact of COVID-19 has only accelerated this generational divide. Remote work became the norm, further highlighting the younger generation's preference for flexibility and blurring the lines between work and personal life. Many individuals across demographics are re-evaluating their priorities, seeking jobs that align with their values and provide a greater sense of purpose—trends exemplified by what's been dubbed the "Great Resignation."

The older generation often views wealth as a slow and steady climb, a ladder where each rung represents years of hard work. The younger generation sees multiple ladders, multiple paths. They're not confined to one job or one identity. They can be consultants, influencers, entre-preneurs, all at once. They are the architects of the gig economy, where flexibility isn't just a perk; it's a fundamental right.

The generational conflicts we witness today are more than mere disagreements about work ethics or life philosophies. They represent a tectonic shift in the way we perceive success, fulfillment, and the very essence of work itself.

For instance, the COVID-19 pandemic served as a catalyst for a significant shift towards remote work and flexible hours. While this move offered numerous benefits, it also highlighted a generational divide regarding work styles and preferences.

We observe a degree of resistance from some older generations who may prefer a return to more traditional work structures, including less flexible hours and a greater emphasis on physical workplace presence. This can create frustration for younger generations who have embraced the advantages of remote work and flexible schedules. The disconnect was starkly illustrated by Zoom, a company synonymous with remote connectivity, requesting employees to return to the office. This seemingly contradictory move highlighted the ongoing tensions between those who favor established work models and those who see value in the new normal.

As we navigate this uncertain terrain, it's vital to recognize that these conflicts are not necessarily negative. They offer opportunities for growth, evolution, and mutual understanding. By embracing the diverse perspectives that different generations offer, we can forge a path that honors both tradition and innovation.

In the end, it's not about choosing one way over the other. Ultimately, it's about recognizing the strengths of each generation and finding a harmonious balance in a complex, multifaceted world. It's a world where flexibility can coexist with commitment, where the gig economy complements traditional employment, and where youthful exuberance finds wisdom in those who paved the way. The dance of contrasts has only just begun.

EMBRACING FULFILLMENT AND DEMOCRATIZING DREAMS IN THE DIGITAL ERA

As a bright-eyed little girl, between the tender ages of five and seven, I would grasp my mother's hands and declare with unshakable certainty, "I want to become a businesswoman." The words resonated in my tiny heart though the real meaning of them eluded my childish understanding. In my innocent mind, I envisioned a life filled with purpose, influence, and financial freedom. The seed of ambition had been planted, even if I had yet to comprehend its full implications.

Life's complex tapestry began to weave its patterns, guiding me down pathways I had never anticipated. Societal norms, familial expectations, the ticking clock of responsibility—all conspired to channel me into a prescribed route. The pursuit of a single full-time occupation was not just the norm but the expectation.

Engineering became my chosen field, consulting my career, and climbing the corporate ladder an all-consuming goal. The victories were sweet, the failures bitter lessons. Yet beneath the surface, a spark remained, a longing for something more. Until one pivotal day, I found myself pausing and demanding of my reflection, "STOP. Wait a minute."

Technology began to play an unexpected role. Social media, once a mere distraction, turned into a doorway to a world brimming with possibilities. Inspirational quotes, motivational videos, professional coaches for physical training, self-publishing schools, marketing guides—everything was suddenly accessible online. I was like Alice tumbling down the rabbit hole, discovering an entirely new world of opportunity.

The realization struck me with profound clarity: I could be so much more. I didn't have to confine myself to one identity or one career. I could be a consultant, an author, a public speaker, a thought leader—the list was endless. And all of it was made possible by technology, the very tool that had once seemed so ordinary.

My story is not just a personal journey but a testament to the transformative power of our Digital Age. And I am sure most people in the same generation are sharing the same feeling. Technology has opened up countless career possibilities. It has allowed us to explore diverse identities, to connect with people across the globe, to learn, to grow, and above all, to dream again.

Have you ever caught yourself feeling nostalgic about those early years? A time when your biggest dream might have been to fly, to explore unknown worlds, or perhaps to be an artist painting with the colors of the wind. While many of us grow up relegating these dreams to the fond vault of childhood memories, it's essential to understand that these very dreams carve out the foundation for our adult ambitions, desires, and overarching sense of purpose.

However, as we evolve, so does the world around us. And in this ever-evolving Digital Age, dreams aren't just fantasies; they are tangible possibilities waiting to be explored. Technology has transcended its role as a mere tool. It has become a bridge to the realization of our most profound aspirations.

Consider, for instance, the realm of virtual reality. A realm that allows a dancer confined to a wheelchair to experience the thrill of a pirouette or an elderly individual to revisit their childhood neighborhood. Similarly, platforms like YouTube, TikTok, and Instagram have transformed passionate individuals into global phenomena. An artist no longer needs a gallery to display their art; a writer doesn't necessarily need a traditional publisher. The digital realm has democratized dreams, allowing for a space where passion, talent, and technology converge to create magic.

Yet, it's essential to remember that technology, in all its glory, is a double-edged sword. While it grants access to limitless opportunities, it also demands self-awareness. It's easy to get caught up in the chaos of virtual possibilities and forget the essence of our true dreams. This is where commitment to yourself becomes paramount.

Commitment in the digital era isn't just about dedicating time or resources. It's about filtering the noise, understanding the genuine from the transient, and, most importantly, staying true to your dreams amidst countless distractions of online influences. It's about discerning which technological tool or platform aligns with your dream, and harnessing it, not as a distraction, but as a catalyst.

And so, as we navigate this exciting digital landscape, the mantra remains simple yet profound: dream as much as you can. Let these dreams, no matter how naive or grand, be your guiding star. With technology at your fingertips and commitment in your heart, the path to personal flourishing is not just a possibility; it's a promise.

In the end, the digital era holds up a mirror, reflecting not just your face but your aspirations, your passions, and your potential. The question is, are you ready to see not just who you are, but all that you can be?

As we stand on the threshold of an era where the only limit is our imagination, I invite you to reflect on your own dreams and the possibilities that await you. Whether it's the young girl with stars in her eyes or the mature woman with a passion for business, your dreams are valid, and they are attainable NOW if you embrace the change.

So, dare to dream, dare to explore, and dare to embrace the multifaceted you. In this boundless world powered by technology, your path is yours to forge. It's never too late to become what you might have been. The journey begins with a single step, a single click, a single leap of faith. Will you take it?

My two take-ways:

- *Dream as much as you can in the digital era.* I promise you will thrive if you commit to yourself. Your dreams lay the foundation for your lifelong pursuits and sense of purpose. Youthful naivety often shapes them, but it's never too late to realize them. Embrace your dreams and let them guide you. Technology is not just a tool but a key to unlocking possibilities previously deemed impossible. If you know how to leverage it, the Digital Age can break down traditional barriers, enabling multifaceted career paths and opportunities for self-exploration.
- *Learn to navigate generational gaps.* The challenges of societal norms, familial pressures, and the unique expectations of our era can divert or even suppress our true passions. Recognizing and overcoming conflicts with older generations might be your only hurdle.

As we transition into Chapter 7 "The IQ Era Ends: Building the Augmented Human Intelligence," it's crucial to consider how we can support future generations in not just surviving but thriving and "dying alive" in a digitally dominated era. If technology has reshaped external success metrics, might it also aid in broadening our understanding of intelligence itself? Moving forward, it is essential to expand our focus beyond mere intellectual quotient (IQ) to encompass emotional (EQ) and spiritual intelligence (SQ). These aspects of intelligence play critical roles in building resilience, fostering meaningful connections, and finding purpose—elements that are as vital as cognitive skills in navigating the complexities of today's world. In the next chapter we will delve into how we can actively enhance these dimensions of intelligence, utilizing technology not just as a tool for information and communication, but as a means to develop deeper emotional understanding and spiritual awareness.

CHAPTER 6 TAKEAWAYS

Technology has become a defining factor of the modern world, particularly for Generations Y and Z. This has led to significant shifts in how they view everything from wellness and careers to travel and spirituality.

Technology has made fulfilling dreams more attainable than ever. The ability to work remotely or build a business online empowers people to live multifaceted lives with greater freedom. But, it requires commitment and focus to filter the digital noise.

The Digital Age brings generational conflicts to the forefront. Older generations may see a methodical, time-intensive approach as synonymous with success while younger generations seek flexibility and the integration of work and personal life.

Generational differences about work, success, and life philosophies are not merely disagreements but a chance for evolution and mutual understanding.

THE IQ ERA ENDS: BUILDING THE AUGMENTED HUMAN INTELLIGENCE

Technology is just a tool. It's a powerful tool, but it's just a tool. Deep human connection is very different. It's not a tool. It's not a means to an end. It is the end—the purpose and the result of a meaningful life, and it will inspire the most amazing acts of love, generosity, and humanity.

—Bill Gates

T he fusion of human sciences and technology is a cornerstone in the evolution of our society. It's through a deep understanding of human thoughts, emotions, and behaviors that we can create technological innovations that transcend mere utility. These advancements not only address practical needs but also enrich our perception of reality, adhering to ethical and moral principles. This fusion ensures that technology acts as a catalyst for an enhanced human experience, one that is beneficial, sustainable, and ethically sound. It establishes a symbiotic relationship between humans and their technological creations, grounded in harmony and mutual enhancement.

However, the true essence of enhancing life quality goes beyond developing convenient technology. It lies in reconnecting with our core human nature, encompassing the entirety of human intelligence. This includes the intellectual, but also the often-neglected spiritual and emotional dimensions. By integrating these elements into technological design, we can significantly reshape our worldview, enriching our interactions with the diverse perspectives that surround us. This approach positions technology as a tool for fostering personal and communal evolution, deepening the human experience in a more comprehensive and profound manner.

A common misconception held by many is that AI's impact on human intelligence will be predominantly in the intellectual realm, with fears centered around knowledge usurpation and job displacement, potentially diminishing intellectual capacities. However, this perspective overlooks the broader, more nuanced implications of AI.

Firstly, AI's integration into various fields does not equate to a direct reduction in human intellectual engagement. Instead, AI often takes over repetitive, laborious tasks, freeing humans to engage in more creative, strategic, and complex problem-solving activities. This shift can actually enhance the intellectual capabilities of individuals by allowing them to focus on tasks that require higher cognitive skills.

Secondly, the advent of AI opens up new avenues for learning and knowledge expansion. AI-driven tools can provide personalized learning experiences, identify knowledge gaps, and offer resources to fill these gaps, thereby contributing to the intellectual growth of individuals.

Furthermore, AI's impact extends beyond the intellectual to emotional and spiritual realms. For instance, advanced AI systems are being developed to recognize and respond to human emotions, potentially offering insights for personal growth or even facilitating therapeutic applications. While many of these applications are still under development and their effectiveness is evolving, their potential is undeniable. This is precisely the area I aim to analyze further.

The quest to understand human intelligence is an exploration into unknown depths. Far beyond mere calculations and logic, our minds are shaped by emotions, intuitions, and a sense of something greater than ourselves. To truly unlock the potential of artificial intelligence in augmenting our own, we must first delve into the hidden patterns of human intelligence. What are the mysterious forces that shape our decisions, drive our creativity, and inspire our search for meaning? If we can decipher these fundamental patterns, we'll ignite a revolution in human potential, harnessing the full power of technology in unlocking and amplifying our intelligence. This is not just an exercise in engineering; it's a journey to uncover the very essence of what makes us human.

HUMAN INTELLIGENCE—A COMPOSITE OF COGNITIVE MASTERY AND EMOTIONAL INSIGHT

Human intelligence is a complex tapestry of cognitive mastery, embodying a person's inherent ability to think, learn, and understand. It's not merely a tool but a combination of abilities enabling us to recognize patterns, innovate, solve problems, make decisions, retain information, and communicate effectively.

This intellectual capacity is multifaceted, encompassing logical reasoning, problem-solving, abstract thinking, and strategic planning. Psychologists view it as crucial for adapting to our environment and tackling abstract challenges. This aligns with This aligns with the perspective of physicist and philosopher Danah Zohar and psychiatrist Ian Marshall's perspective, emphasizing human intelligence as a key behavioral trait in modern society, by researchers like John L. Gould and Carol Grant Gould who see it as essential for success in life.[1]

The introduction of multiple intelligences by developmental psychologist Howard Gardner marks a paradigm shift in our understanding of intellectual capacity. Gardner's model breaks intelligence into various forms, revealing a spectrum of human talents and abilities.

Central to this is the triad of intelligence types: the intelligence quotient (IQ), emotional quotient (EQ), and spiritual quotient (SQ). IQ assesses analytical and logical skills, EQ gauges our ability to understand and manage emotions (ours and others'), and SQ measures our inner balance and depth of life understanding. Collectively, they create a nuanced framework of human intelligence.

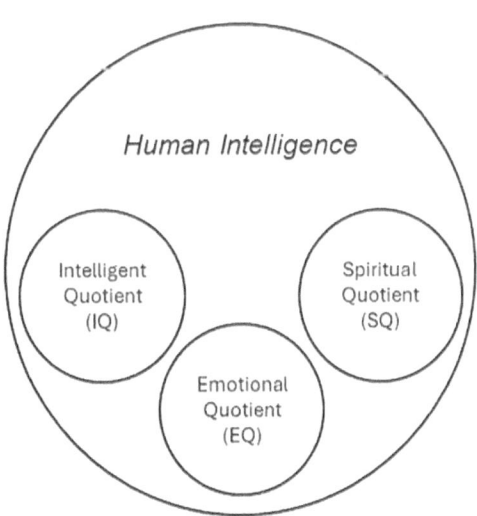

However, there's a prevailing overemphasis on IQ in much of the world today, often seen as the sole measure of intelligence for many years. This narrow focus can lead to dissatisfaction since intellectual intelligence alone doesn't guarantee happiness or success in navigating life's complexities. In fact, a high IQ without balanced EQ and SQ can result in difficulties integrating into society. Statistically, this imbalance is concerning: a study by the National Institute of Health found that individuals with very high IQs (130 or above) are more prone to social anxiety disorders.[2]

This suggests that high IQ individuals may struggle with emotional regulation and understanding, a deficiency in EQ. While less direct statistical evidence exists for SQ, studies indicate that higher SQ is associated with better life satisfaction and mental health outcomes.[3] Statistically, this imbalance concerns numerous geniuses with high IQs but low EQ and SQ. Scores often experience depression and suicidal tendencies. This highlights the importance of a holistic approach to intelligence, valuing all aspects equally for a well-rounded and fulfilling life.

These diverse intelligences, while anatomically separate, often work together, with each influencing the others. Despite this, a common misconception equates IQ with overall intelligence, neglecting the equally important emotional and spiritual aspects. Intriguingly, IQ statistics reveal fascinating trends, especially when looking at generational shifts. The Flynn effect, named after psychologist James R. Flynn, indicates that IQ scores have been increasing worldwide for decades. For instance, average IQ scores in the United States increased three points every decade since the early 20th century.[4] This upward trend suggests improvements in education, nutrition, and overall living conditions, underscoring the environmental impact on cognitive development.

Additionally, recent studies suggest a reversal of the Flynn effect in some countries, with average IQ scores declining since the mid-1990s.[5] Factors like changes in educational policies, shifts in media consumption, and environmental influences are speculated to contribute to this decline.

To illustrate this more, global comparisons of IQ scores reveal significant disparities. For instance, East Asian countries like Japan and South Korea typically score higher on average compared to other regions. These variations reflect not only genetic factors but also differences in culture, education, and socioeconomic conditions.

This expanded understanding of IQ, its determinants, and implications emphasizes the need for a more nuanced approach to intelligence. It's not merely a measure of cognitive ability but a complex interplay of environmental, emotional, and societal factors. As we evolve in our understanding of intelligence, the role of IQ must be contextualized within this broader, more holistic framework, recognizing its limitations and the importance of other forms of intelligence in determining success and adaptability in an ever-changing world.

Now that we understand the interconnectedness of these three forms of intelligence, the remainder of the chapter will explore each in more detail. We'll also examine how technology and AI have the potential to influence and enhance these three forms of intelligence.

INTELLIGENCE QUOTIENT (IQ) BEYOND TRADITIONAL COGNITIVE MEASURES

The intelligence quotient, or IQ, stands as a crucial but debated component in the realm of intelligence theory. Defining intelligence itself is a challenge, with varied interpretations across academia. Scholars such as psychologist Ulric Neisser, cognitive scientist Robert Sternberg, and cognitive psychologist Steven Pinker conceptualize intelligence as the capacity for goal achievement, navigating obstacles through rational and logical decision-making.[6] In contrast, social psychologists Chi-yue Chiu, Ying-yi Hong, and Carol Dweck view it as the level of skills and knowledge available for problem-solving.[7]

Robert A. Emmons a well-known psychologist broadens this perspective, identifying specific intelligence domains like the scope of knowledge, achievement in performance, adaptability under challenging conditions, creativity, and the pace of learning and adaptation.[8] In organizational settings, particularly human resource development (HRD), IQ is often paramount. It encompasses the development of employee skills and logical abilities and knowledge, deemed crucial for career advancement.

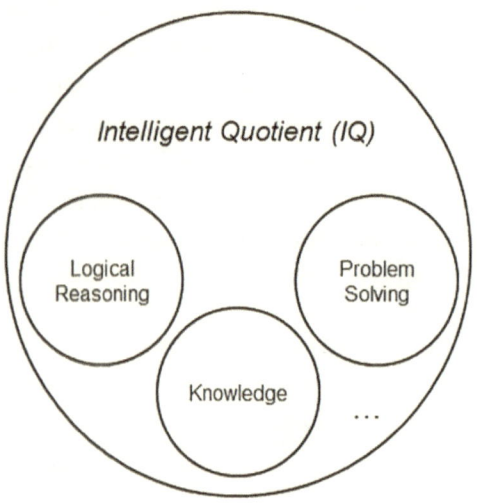

One of the most effective ways to develop our IQ is through education. Yet, as we stand at the cusp of a technological revolution, traditional educational models give way to a future where learning and intelligence augmentation merge seamlessly with the digital world. Recent findings, like the 2018 meta-analysis by Ritchie and Tucker-Drob,[9] definitively establish education's lasting impact on intelligence. It highlighted education as the "most consistent, robust, and durable method" for raising intelligence. When we talk about education, we are not confined to the four walls of a classroom; it encompasses digital platforms, wearable technology like the Apple Watch, virtual assistants, AI tools like GPT, and a plethora of interactive assets.

The fundamental issue with our current educational models lies in their ephemeral nature. Decades of research show that students forget a significant amount of learned material within a few years, a phenomenon known as the "forgetting curve."[10] This isn't simply a matter of too many courses; it's about the mismatch between how we're wired to learn and the rote memorization that often dominates traditional classrooms. Some students thrive on visual representations, others on understanding the underlying logic, yet many educational systems still force all minds into a single framework.

Let's use a physics example: imagine teaching forces not through dry formulas on a board but through immersive VR experiences. You don't just learn about forces; you feel them. You manipulate them, observe their effects, and see the underlying principles unfold in dynamic scenarios. This isn't about mere entertainment; it's about aligning learning with how our brains evolved—through experience and interaction. This kind of learning creates rich neural networks, not easily forgotten facts, but deeply ingrained understanding.

The impact on long-term retention is profound. Traditional memorization-based learning may suffice for a test, but it's like building on an unstable foundation—knowledge fades with time. Experiential learning, made possible through emerging technologies, is like building with stone. It creates a durable foundation of knowledge students can use and expand upon across their lives. This isn't about replacing books entirely, but about a multi-faceted approach that caters to diverse cognitive styles and ensures knowledge becomes a part of who students are, not just what they memorize.

The pace of technological progress suggests a future where education is a seamless, ongoing journey. Wearable augmented reality (AR) overlays could transform our world into a dynamic learning space. A simple walk in the park could become a botany lesson, where AI analyzes plant life as you stroll.

Consider the potential of personalized learning. Imagine AI-powered systems evolving beyond homework helpers into true learning companions, available 24/7, adapting to your unique cognitive patterns, not just tailoring content delivery but optimizing the learning process itself. These systems will act as intelligent guides, constantly analyzing your progress and adjusting their teaching strategies to maximize your IQ gains. Information access has already seen a seismic shift—the internet places the collective wisdom of humanity at our fingertips. Next-generation interfaces, potentially even direct neural links, could transcend search bars and screens, making vast knowledge an extension of our own thought processes.

Technology isn't simply about information delivery—it's about unlocking new modes of learning. Interactive and engaging tools, from simulations to virtual reality experiences, transform abstract concepts into tangible, memorable encounters. Educational games, infused with nuanced problem-solving and real-world scenarios, foster the development of the strategic and analytical skills so central to IQ measurement. This isn't mere gamification, but the creation of intelligently designed environments where practice becomes not a chore, but an exciting journey of self-discovery.

The exponential nature of technological progress holds a profound promise for IQ development. Just as computing power follows Moore's law (discussed in Chapter 12), the sophistication of adaptive learning software will also advance rapidly. The boundaries between traditional classrooms and immersive online learning will dissolve, as augmented reality overlays our physical environments with dynamic educational experiences. This transcends mere access to knowledge—it fosters a learning mindset embedded in daily life.

EMOTIONAL QUOTIENT (EQ): EVOLVING PERSPECTIVES AND GENERATIONAL SHIFTS

Emotional quotient (EQ) has emerged as a pivotal element in understanding human intelligence, transcending traditional cognitive assessments. Initially introduced by psychologists Peter Salovey and John D. Mayer in 1990, EQ encapsulates the ability to recognize, comprehend, and manage one's own emotions and those of others. This concept, popularized by Daniel Goleman's influential work *Emotional Intelligence*, positioned EQ as a critical factor in personal and professional domains, surpassing the conventional bounds of IQ. Salovey and Mayer further refined EQ as encompassing mental abilities directly linked to emotional processing.

The evolution of EQ over generations presents intriguing insights, reflecting societal, technological, and educational shifts. Interestingly, unlike IQ, which has quantifiable metrics like the Flynn effect, the progression of EQ is more nuanced and less linear, influenced by complex social dynamics.

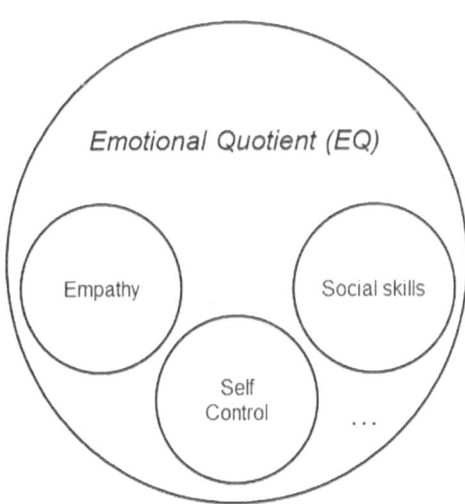

A significant development in the realm of emotional quotient (EQ) is the positive influence of digitalization and social media on facets such as empathy and social awareness. Contrary to concerns about digital communication diminishing interpersonal skills, there's evidence suggesting an enhancement in these areas. For instance, the American Psychological Association observed a notable rise in social sensitivity among younger generations, a trend believed to be linked to their increased exposure to diverse global narratives and social justice themes through online platforms.[11]

This increase in empathy and social consciousness is not just anecdotal. A research study found that social media users, especially in younger demographics, exhibited higher levels of empathy, likely due to their engagement with a variety of human experiences and viewpoints shared online.[12] Another study found that social support and empathy are "contagious," with users who received support in their first post more likely to continue posting and support others, and those receiving empathic support subsequently expressing higher levels of empathy in online mental health communities.[13]

Additionally, the Digital Empathy Project, a research initiative examining the impact of digital communication on empathy, revealed that digital platforms could act as effective tools for empathy education and development.[14] Their findings indicated that structured digital interactions, like collaborative online learning or social media-based discussion groups, significantly improved participants' ability to understand and share the feelings of others.

The evolution of EQ in the Digital Age isn't just about organic social interactions—it's about harnessing technology as a deliberate tool for emotional growth. From targeted applications to immersive experiences, we're seeing the emergence of a powerful new ecosystem of EQ-focused technologies.

Modern educational systems, increasingly acknowledging the importance of EQ, have begun integrating social and emotional learning

(SEL) into curricula. This shift is in response to studies, like one from the Collaborative for Academic, Social, and Emotional Learning (CASEL), showing that students participating in SEL programs demonstrated an 11% increase in academic achievement scores.[15] These interactive programs provide structured lessons not only on empathy and understanding others, but also on crucial skills like self-awareness, stress management, and conflict resolution. Imagine personalized modules teaching self-calming techniques for moments of anxiety or interactive simulations where users practice navigating disagreements with virtual peers. AI-powered personalization is becoming a game-changer in this field, allowing these apps to tailor activities and feedback to individual users' needs, maximizing their impact on managing emotions and resolving conflicts constructively.

Virtual reality (VR) and simulations hold unique promise for developing a wide range of EQ skills. Stepping into the shoes of someone with a vastly different life experience is now possible with VR. Imagine embodying a firefighter in a high-pressure rescue situation or a business leader negotiating a complex deal. Such simulations cultivate a deep, embodied understanding of emotions, how to manage them under pressure, and the crucial role of self-control in decision-making.

Beyond targeted apps and experiences, everyday communication platforms can themselves become EQ training grounds. Moderated online discussions and collaborative projects require effective communication, teamwork, and the ability to navigate disagreements respectfully. AI-powered tools can even offer real-time feedback on users' communication styles, suggesting ways to be more assertive, manage stress through difficult conversations, and navigate conflict resolution in a mature and constructive manner.

Of course, technology is only a tool, and its effectiveness depends on proper integration. Teachers and parents must be equipped to guide children's use of these resources. Further research is needed to determine the long-term impact, and we must address issues of access, ensuring these technologies are available to all. Nevertheless, the potential is transformative, offering promising avenues for fostering a more empathetic and socially conscious generation.

SPIRITUAL INTELLIGENCE (SQ): EVOLVING UNDERSTANDING AND ITS IMPACT

Spiritual intelligence (SQ) has increasingly been recognized as a vital component of overall well-being and decision-making, intertwining the realms of spirituality and cognitive function. Cynthia Miller-Perrin and Elisabeth Mancuso, both distinguished psychologists, have underscored the significant role spirituality plays in enhancing well-being and mental health in leading a meaningful life.[16] Spiritual traditions across the globe have long advocated for the cultivation of a "pure heart," a state believed to enhance decision-making beyond what intellect or reason alone can achieve. This approach posits that the spiritual self taps into a higher wisdom, offering deep insights and realizations.

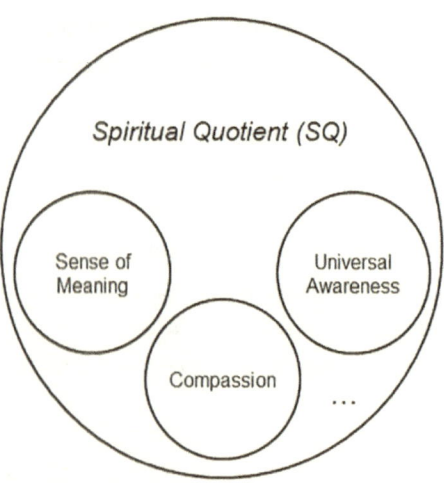

The practical application of spirituality in addressing real-world challenges has drawn attention in the business world. Entrepreneurs, managers, and leaders are increasingly recognizing the value of spirituality in problem-solving and goal attainment. Spiritual intelligence is now being considered a legitimate and predictive form of intelligence in various sectors, including business, as per the economist and professor Saeid Taghizadeh Yazdi and the political scientist Timothy Sisk.[17]

Howard Gardner's multiple intelligences theory, first presented in 1983, initially did not include spirituality but later adaptations and research, including Gardner's own reflections in 2000, suggested incorporating existential and moral intelligence into the framework. This inclusion acknowledges spirituality as a cognitive process that helps individuals comprehend and enhance their lives.

Statistics and trends in SQ present a fascinating picture. Research by the Pew Research Center shows that millennials are more likely to identify as spiritual rather than religious, with over 60% reporting that they feel a deep sense of spiritual peace and well-being at least weekly.[18] This shift from organized religion to personal spirituality indicates a growing trend in seeking meaning and understanding beyond traditional religious frameworks.

Furthermore, a study by the American Psychological Association found that individuals who engage in regular spiritual practices display higher levels of happiness and mental well-being.[19] This is particularly evident in younger generations who prioritize personal growth and self-understanding.

Educational systems are also increasingly acknowledging the importance of SQ. A survey by the Association for Supervision and Curriculum Development found that schools in the United States now include some form of spiritual or moral education in their curricula, recognizing its role in holistic development.[20]

The potential extends beyond personal practice. Imagine technology enhancing how we teach about spiritual and philosophical concepts in the classroom. Interactive presentations, VR experiences that transport students to historical sites of spiritual significance, or AI-powered discussion platforms that allow safe and structured explorations of diverse belief systems—these could cultivate a greater appreciation for SQ's role in shaping human experience.

One of the most striking trends in the rise of SQ is the growing popularity of meditation and mindfulness apps among younger users. A report by Statista revealed that in 2021, the global mindfulness meditation apps market was valued at approximately 4.2 billion US dollars, with a significant portion of the users being millennials and Gen Z.[21] Apps like Headspace and Calm have seen a surge in subscriptions, with Headspace reporting over 65 million users in 2020, a substantial number of whom are under the age of 35. This indicates a shift towards digital tools for spiritual development and a greater emphasis on mental health and well-being among younger people.

Social media and online platforms have also played a pivotal role in this increase in spiritual engagement. Platforms like YouTube, Instagram, and TikTok have seen a rise in content related to spirituality, mindfulness, and personal growth. A survey conducted by the Global Web Index in 2019 found that 25% of internet users ages 16 to 24 follow content related to mindfulness and spirituality on social media, indicating a growing interest in these areas.[22]

Moreover, the connection between spiritual practices and longer lifespans has been the subject of several studies. Research published in the journal *JAMA Internal Medicine* found that people who regularly engage in meditation and spiritual practices have a lower mortality rate.[23] The study concluded that those who meditated regularly had a 30% lower risk of mortality compared to those who did not. Another study found that individuals with high levels of spiritual well-being, including a sense of peace and meaning in life, exhibited lower levels of inflammation, a key factor in numerous chronic diseases and conditions associated with aging.[24]

In conclusion, the increasing recognition and integration of SQ across various domains reflects a broader societal shift towards valuing inner wisdom and moral understanding. This trend, driven by a move away from organized religion towards personal spirituality, is evident in younger generations' approach to life and well-being. The growing emphasis on SQ in education and business sectors underscores its importance not just in personal growth but also in fostering ethical, empathetic, and socially responsible individuals. The evolution of SQ highlights a collective journey towards deeper self-awareness and a more profound understanding of our place in the world.

However, it's crucial to acknowledge that technology is a tool, not a replacement for direct experience. Excessive screen time can undermine the very mindfulness we seek to cultivate. Additionally, there's the risk of prioritizing online spiritual content over in-person spiritual communities or traditional practices with deep historical roots. Instead, technology must be seen as a supplement, a gateway to further self-exploration and real-world connections.

The most transformative potential lies in integrating technologies into a holistic approach to education. Just as we strive for IQ and EQ development, fostering SQ should hold equal importance. This means using technology not just to teach facts but to create experiences that spark introspection, promote ethical thinking, and guide students in finding their own sense of purpose in a complex world.

As we close Chapter 7, we've examined the limitations of a purely IQ-focused approach and highlighted the importance of emotional and spiritual intelligence—often neglected aspects of well-being and interpersonal effectiveness that technology can significantly impact. This chapter explored how we can leverage technology to cultivate these intelligences, yet a question remains: can technology offer more than just tools for enhancement and support? Imagine a future where technology doesn't just empower us to sharpen our existing intelligences but actually augments our brains themselves. Chapter 8 dives into this fascinating possibility, exploring the world of brain-computer interfaces and mind-machine merging. As we explore the potential to directly enhance human capabilities, we also confront the ethical, practical, and societal implications of such profound advancements.

CHAPTER 7 TAKEAWAYS

Intelligence isn't just about IQ. It's a complex tapestry of intellectual capacity (IQ), emotional understanding (EQ), and spiritual depth (SQ). Here's what we know:

IQ is not everything. IQ remains important for problem-solving and learning. However, high IQ alone doesn't guarantee happiness or balanced living.

EQ is the key to connection. Understanding and handling our own emotions, and those of others, is crucial for strong relationships and navigating complexity.

SQ is about finding inner wisdom. Spirituality, whether through traditional religion or personal practices, contributes to well-being, decision-making, and a sense of meaning.

Education remains the bedrock of IQ. To boost your IQ, explore interactive learning platforms, AR, and VR for immersive, engaging experiences that promote deeper understanding and knowledge retention.

To enhance your EQ practice active listening, empathy, and self-awareness techniques. Technology can aid this: utilize apps focused on conflict resolution, communication skills, and managing emotional triggers.

To nurture your SQ explore mindfulness, meditation apps, and diverse spiritual/philosophical content. Seek out enriching discussions and connect with like-minded individuals.

THE QUEST FOR HUMAN-EQUIVALENT COMPUTING

As I discuss in Engines of Creation, *if you can build genuine AI, there are reasons to believe that you can build things like neurons that are a million times faster. That leads to the conclusion that you can make systems that think a million times faster than a person.*

—Eric Drexler, engineer and author

I n the previous chapter, we embarked on a journey to redefine intelligence itself. We explored how technology and the potential of IQ, EQ, and SQ can converge, unlocking the boundless possibilities within the human mind. In this chapter we will explore a world where advancements in fields like nanotechnology, biotechnology, and even the manipulation of light itself have the potential to augment our capacities like never before. Imagine technologies that seamlessly enhance not just our minds, but also our capacity for empathy, compassion, and ethical understanding. The result is not merely a smarter world, but one imbued with a depth of human connection and moral awareness previously unimaginable.

But how does this all work in real life? How can we actually connect our brains to computers? What's going on in the world of computer technology today? What big challenges are out there, and what should we think about to make sure we're using this technology the right way?

Imagine a young inventor in the year 2040 who created a connected device that translates animals' emotions into recognizable sounds. Initially, it's fun to "hear" their playful thoughts. But later, the device reveals the sadness of farm animals, their sounds filled with fear and discomfort. The inventor suddenly faces a difficult choice. On one hand, their technology could expose how these animals feel, potentially leading to big changes in how they are raised, ensuring better conditions. Yet, on the other hand, this same discovery could cause people to get angry at the meat industry, potentially leading to self-reflection or even disgust among meat-eaters.

This story helps us think about what we'll cover in this chapter. We'll look at how close we are to truly connecting our minds with machines. What new things in computer technology are helping us get there? And what big questions do we need to answer to use this technology responsibly?

We'll explore questions like:

- How far have we come in merging our minds with machines?
- What new advances in computer technology are making this possible?
- What should we be careful about as we bring together our minds and machines?

As we explore these questions, we'll see that the future isn't just one place we're going to. It's shaped by our choices, the new things we create, and how we handle important questions.

But the story doesn't end with just connecting our minds to computers. There's so much more to think about. How will this technology affect our daily lives? How will it change how we work, learn, and communicate with one another? What about our privacy and freedom? These are big questions that we need to think about carefully.

Let's also think about the people who might not have access to this technology. How will it affect them? Will it create a bigger gap between people who have a lot and those who don't?

We'll also look at how this technology can help people with disabilities. Imagine being able to speak using only your thoughts or controlling a computer without moving a muscle. This could open up a whole new world for many people.

NANOBOTS, NEURONS, AND THE FUTURE OF THE MIND

In our exploration of the future of brain technology, we are entering a transformative era where the fusion of biology and technology could revolutionize human intelligence. Have you ever wondered what it would be like to remember every detail of your life or solve complex problems in seconds? Visionaries like computer scientist, author, inventor, and futurist Ray Kurzweil have not only wondered but have also paved the way for such possibilities, where our cognitive functions are not just replicated but enhanced by advances in artificial intelligence and neuroscience.

Consider for a moment the intricacy of the human brain. It's a marvel of nature, yet we're on the brink of augmenting its capabilities. It reminds me of the first time I tried to disassemble a watch; I could take it apart and put it back together, but understanding how to enhance its functionality was another challenge.

Understanding the complexity of the human brain is crucial as we advance in this field. There are valid concerns about whether we fully comprehend the engineering principles enough to improve it. Despite these concerns, the progress in brain research is noteworthy. Scientists are doing extensive research in the brain but are understanding it through methodical exploration, supported by increasingly sophisticated models and high-quality data.

Imagine a world where diseases like Alzheimer's or Parkinson's are no longer life sentences, where breakthroughs in brain research provide hope and solutions. Every year, brain scanning technologies double in their resolution and capabilities. This rapid advancement is not just a statistic; it's a beacon of hope for better understanding and treating brain disorders. Think about the potential impact on education, healthcare, and even our daily lives.

In 2005, when Kurzweil predicted in his book *The Singularity Is Near* the advent of nanobots for brain exploration in the 2020s, it sounded like science fiction. Yet, here we are in 2023, on the cusp of making such technologies a reality. Although nanobots exploring our brains like tiny astronauts is still in development, the research in nanotechnology is progressing rapidly. These advancements are not just scientific achievements; they represent a future where our health and well-being are significantly improved.

The development of nanobots for medical use is particularly intriguing. Imagine sending microscopic robots to repair cells or map brain activity.

It's like having a team of microscopic doctors inside you, constantly working to keep you healthy. In 2016, the nanomedicine market was valued at approximately $138.8 billion, and it's projected to reach $351 billion by 2025.[1] This growth isn't just financial; it represents a paradigm shift in how we approach medicine and health.

The potential of nanobots in diagnosing and treating neurological conditions is especially promising. The ability to cross the blood-brain barrier, a game-changer once thought impossible, could revolutionize the treatment of neurological diseases. This isn't just about technological advancement; it's about giving hope to millions who suffer from these conditions.

CURRENT LANDSCAPE OF COMPUTATIONAL TECHNOLOGY
1—Computing with Nanotubes

In the realm of technological evolution, few advancements captivate the imagination quite like the promise of nanotubes. Ray Kurzweil, in his visionary work *The Singularity Is Near*, emphasizes this groundbreaking technology, underscoring its potential to revolutionize computing. As we unpack this concept, let's journey through the landscape of nanotubes, understanding their significance and potential in reshaping our technological future.

Nanotubes are tiny tubes, just one nanometer wide, made from carbon atoms. They're so small that you could fit about 50,000 of them across the width of a human hair. Despite their size, they are incredibly important for the future of technology. Here's why: these nanotubes can store and process information, just like the chips in our computers and phones. But they can do it much smaller and much faster. Imagine your current computer or smartphone being thousands of times faster. That's what nanotubes could make possible.

In the early 2000s, scientists started making big breakthroughs with nanotubes. They found ways to use them in transistors (tiny switches that are the building blocks of electronics) and in computer memory. The most exciting part? These nanotube transistors can work super fast, theoretically up to a thousand times faster than today's computers.

But there were challenges. Nanotubes tend to grow in messy, random ways, which makes it hard to use them in precise electronics. Over time, researchers figured out how to line them up properly. For example, IBM found a way to grow nanotubes in an orderly fashion, a bit like how we make silicon chips today.

Now, think about the impact of this. With nanotube technology, we could make computers that are not only faster but also much smaller. This could change everything from how we use personal devices to how we handle big data, which could contribute to finding solutions for complex problems like climate change or medical research.

2—Computing with Molecules

The idea here is about using individual molecules to do computing tasks. This might sound like science fiction, but scientists have been thinking about this since the 1970s. But at that time, we didn't have the right technology to make it happen. We needed better electronics, a deeper understanding of physics and chemistry, and even some insights from biology to start turning this idea into reality.

Fast forward to 2002, scientists found a way to add or remove a single silicon atom from a group of atoms. This is very precise work, done with a special tool called a scanning tunneling microscope. The exciting part? This method could store way more data than current hard drives—we're talking about millions of times more data in the same amount of space.

Then there's the speed of these molecular computing systems. A researcher named Peter Burke predicted that these systems could reach speeds of one terahertz. To put that in perspective, it's way faster than the best computers we have today. And this prediction seems to be on track. Scientists at the University of Illinois at Urbana-Champaign created a tiny transistor that operates at over 600 gigahertz—that's more than half a terahertz.

A particularly interesting molecule for this kind of computing is called "rotaxane." It can switch between different states, which is crucial for computing, by changing the energy in a part of the molecule that looks like a ring. Researchers have already shown that this rotaxane can be used for memory and switching in electronic devices. They've demonstrated that it can store a huge amount of data—100 gigabits per square inch. And they think it could store even more if we arrange these molecules in three dimensions, not just flat on a surface.

In simple terms, computing with molecules is about using the smallest parts of matter—molecules and atoms—to store and process information. This could lead to computers that are much smaller, faster, and have way more storage than anything we have now. But it's not just about computers—molecular machines could revolutionize other fields too. Imagine tiny medical devices delivering drugs right where they're needed, electronics built with molecular switches, or even flexible materials that mimic muscles. It's still early days, but this technology has the potential to completely transform how we use computers in the future.

3—Computing with DNA

DNA computing is an innovative way of using the DNA molecule. It doesn't use traditional electronic components. Instead, it leverages the properties of DNA—the same molecules that make up our genes. Think of DNA as nature's own version of a nano-computer. Scientists have figured out how to use these tiny natural structures to solve complex problems, much like a computer does.

Imagine a test tube filled with water and trillions of DNA molecules. Each of these DNA molecules acts like a tiny computer. They're not computers in the way we usually think of them; there are no screens or keyboards. Instead, they work at a molecular level.

To solve a problem, scientists create a strand of DNA for each part of the problem, using a special code. These strands are then copied many times over. When these strands are put into the test tube, they naturally start joining together. The way they join can represent different solutions to the problem. The test tube now contains trillions of DNA strands, each a possible solution. To find the correct solution, scientists add special chemicals that remove any DNA strands that don't meet the criteria for a correct answer. This process is repeated until only the DNA strands that represent the correct solution are left.

In theory, DNA computing could be applied to climate prediction by modeling complex climate systems. For this application, scientists could design DNA strands to represent various climatic factors, such as temperature, precipitation levels, atmospheric pressure, and carbon dioxide concentrations. Each strand could be coded to interact based on established climatic models that predict how these factors influence one another under different conditions.

By combining these strands in a test tube, they could potentially form patterns or sequences that reflect the outcomes of different climate scenarios. For example, adding specific enzymes or molecules could trigger reactions among the DNA strands that mimic the effects of increasing greenhouse gases or changing ocean temperatures. To isolate the correct predictions, scientists would then introduce markers or chemicals to bind to or remove DNA strands that do not align with known or expected outcomes based on the climate models. This selective process is repeated until only the strands that represent the most accurate climate predictions remain. The resulting DNA patterns could then be analyzed to predict climate trends or extreme weather events based on how the strands interact.

However, there are significant challenges to realizing this application. Climate systems are extraordinarily complex and involve variables that are continuously changing and interacting in non-linear ways. DNA computing, while powerful for certain types of problems, may not yet have the capacity to handle the dynamic and vast scale of data required for accurate climate modeling.

Currently, all the DNA strands need to work on the same problem at the same time. This makes DNA computers great for certain types of problems but not suited for tasks where different calculations need to be done independently at the same time.

However, it can be useful for specific cases. In a research study titled "Prediction of Radiation Fog by DNA Computing," the researchers proposed using a wet lab algorithm for prediction of radiation fog by DNA computing and obtained satisfactory results at the end of the experiment.[2] This example demonstrates the potential of DNA computing in specialized areas of meteorology where the conditions and required computations are specific and less variable.

In short, DNA computing is an exciting field where biology meets technology. By using the molecular structure of DNA, scientists are exploring new ways to process information, offering a glimpse into a future where computing could be faster and more efficient than ever before.

4—Computing with Light

Optical computing is an innovative approach that uses light, particularly laser beams, to process data. This method is a departure from traditional computing, which relies on electrical signals. In optical computing, information is carried in streams of photons, which are particles of light. Think of it like traditional computers using electrical signals to represent data, but instead, optical computers use light.

The process involves various optical components such as lenses and mirrors to manipulate these beams of light. These components can direct, split, combine, and control the light in ways that enable the performance of logical and arithmetic operations on the data encoded within the light beams.

Lenslet, an Israeli company, demonstrates the potential of computing with light. Their system uses 256 lasers, each carrying a unique data stream. It can perform an astounding eight trillion calculations per second by working on all these data streams at once. Imagine a super-efficient assembly line where each worker handles a different task simultaneously. This technology is particularly promising for video processing, potentially allowing real-time compression of hundreds of video channels at once.

In essence, computing with light represents a significant shift from the traditional electronic computing paradigm. It utilizes the unique properties of light for high-speed data processing and opens up new avenues in the field of computing, especially for tasks that benefit from high-speed, repetitive processing. For example, optical systems have the potential to revolutionize data centers, handling our internet searches and online activity with unprecedented speed. Complex scientific simulations, like modeling weather patterns, could run at incredible speeds on light-based computers, leading to breakthroughs in our understanding of the world. Artificial intelligence could also benefit, with image recognition and other tasks happening so fast that self-driving cars and AI assistants react in real time. Lastly, optical computing might lead to ultra-secure communication networks, transmitting data through light beams that are much harder to intercept than electronic signals.

These advancements mark a pivotal moment in the evolution of computing, signaling a new era in our quest for human transformation and transcendence. While challenges remain, the potential benefits are profound and far-reaching. As these technologies continue to mature, they promise to revolutionize various sectors, enhancing efficiency and expanding the boundaries of what's possible. In doing so, they not only improve our capabilities but also offer new pathways for us to explore the very essence of what it means to be human.

LIMITS OF COMPUTATION AND OTHER CONSIDERATIONS

In our ongoing quest to comprehend the limits of computational power, we stand at the intersection of physics and information technology, a junction where the potential of our computing future is as vast as the universe itself.

While the theoretical computational power of matter seems limitless, there are real-world constraints to consider. As Ray Kurzweil notes, the quest to maximize processing power forces us to confront the very laws of physics. Einstein's iconic equation $E=mc^2$ tells us that the energy contained in even a small amount of matter is immense, due to the speed of light squared being so vast. Combining this with Planck's constant (6.6 x 10^-34 joule-seconds), the smallest unit of energy we can use for computation, reveals the theoretical limits of computational power.

These limits, however, don't diminish the awe-inspiring possibilities they imply. Imagine a hypothetical laptop operating at these absolute physical limits. Kurzweil calculates it could perform roughly 5 x 10^{50} operations per second—equivalent to the combined brainpower of billions of human civilizations! That's the power to process the equivalent of ten thousand years of human thought in less than a nanosecond.

Of course, achieving this in practice faces obstacles. Converting a whole laptop's mass into energy for computing would unleash destructive force comparable to a thermonuclear explosion, clearly undesirable. Additionally, reaching the theoretical memory density Kurzweil envisions poses practical limitations we're still working to overcome.

Despite these hurdles, we keep pushing those limits. Storing 50 bits on a single atom is already achievable, though on a limited scale. New technologies might let us use an atom's spin, position, and other quantum properties for even denser storage. This journey is step by step. Each advance unlocks further advances, propelling us closer to the theoretical limits. Looking ahead, Kurzweil forecasts a future where 10^{42} operations per second could be accessible in a portable device by 2080. Such a machine could simulate millennia of human thought, for a reasonable cost. Alternative paths exist too: Eric Drexler's patented nanotechnology design, a mechanical nano computer, could theoretically simulate hundreds of thousands of brains in the space of a sugar cube.

These possibilities come with a crucial caveat. As computing power reaches unprecedented heights, ethical concerns arise. Technology capable of such profound advancements must be developed alongside careful consideration of its potential for both good and harm.

We must tread with caution when considering their human and economic consequences. Take, for instance, the story mentioned earlier about a device that translates animal emotions. Unveiling the suffering of farm animals could lead to revolutionary reforms, but also spark anger and disrupt entire industries. Such negative consequences are a natural part of major change and shouldn't deter us from progress. It's often upheaval that paves the way for a better future, benefiting generations to come. While it can be unsettling to challenge the status quo and disrupt established industries, we should not fear evolution. History shows us that it's often through these periods of upheaval that we make some of our greatest strides toward a more just and compassionate future. For instance, think of the anti-nuclear movement that gained momentum in the 1960s and the climate change movement, which has seen significant global action since the Paris Agreement in 2015. Let us embrace these challenges, recognizing that they pave the way for progress that benefits generations to come.

But also, success in this technological revolution won't come from technical brilliance alone. We need to seriously question our values. Do we want innovation no matter what the cost? Or do we aim for a future where technology improves everyone's lives and is used responsibly? Future generations, including Generations Y, Z, and beyond, hold incredible power to shape the world. It's thrilling, but also a big responsibility. Technology is not destiny. We shape our destiny—as Brynjolfsson and McAfee highlighted. We must use it wisely, making sure it benefits all of humanity, not just a select few.

Building on these groundbreaking advancements, we've glimpsed the incredible potential that these technologies hold for enhancing human capabilities. As we marvel at these achievements, it's natural to ponder what could be next. What if we take this potential and apply it on a grand scale to develop a Universal Intelligence? Chapter 9, "Universal Intelligence," embarks on this thought-provoking journey. It imagines the possibility of utilizing these sophisticated technologies to forge a comprehensive system of intelligence—one that can seamlessly integrate and analyze the vast expanse of human knowledge. The promise of this Universal Intelligence is not only to enhance our cognitive capacities but also to enrich our collective human experience, guiding us toward a more "alive" life—an enlightened, inclusive, and harmonious understanding of our world.

CHAPTER 8 TAKEAWAYS

We're on the verge of a revolution where biology and technology merge, potentially enhancing our brains. While full understanding of the brain remains a challenge, progress in neuroscience and brain-scanning technologies is rapid, offering hope for treating neurological disorders and possibly enhancing our cognitive functions.

The development of nanorobots for medical use is particularly exciting. These microscopic devices could repair cells, deliver targeted treatment, and revolutionize our approach to health and disease.

Ray Kurzweil's predictions about new forms of computing are becoming reality in terms of nanotubes, molecules and DNA, and optical computing.

Theoretical limits of computation suggest the potential to simulate millennia of human thought in a blink, but this level of power raises complex ethical questions we need to address now.

This technological revolution presents incredible potential and profound responsibility. We must guide it with wisdom to ensure it enhances human well-being and creates a future we want to live in.

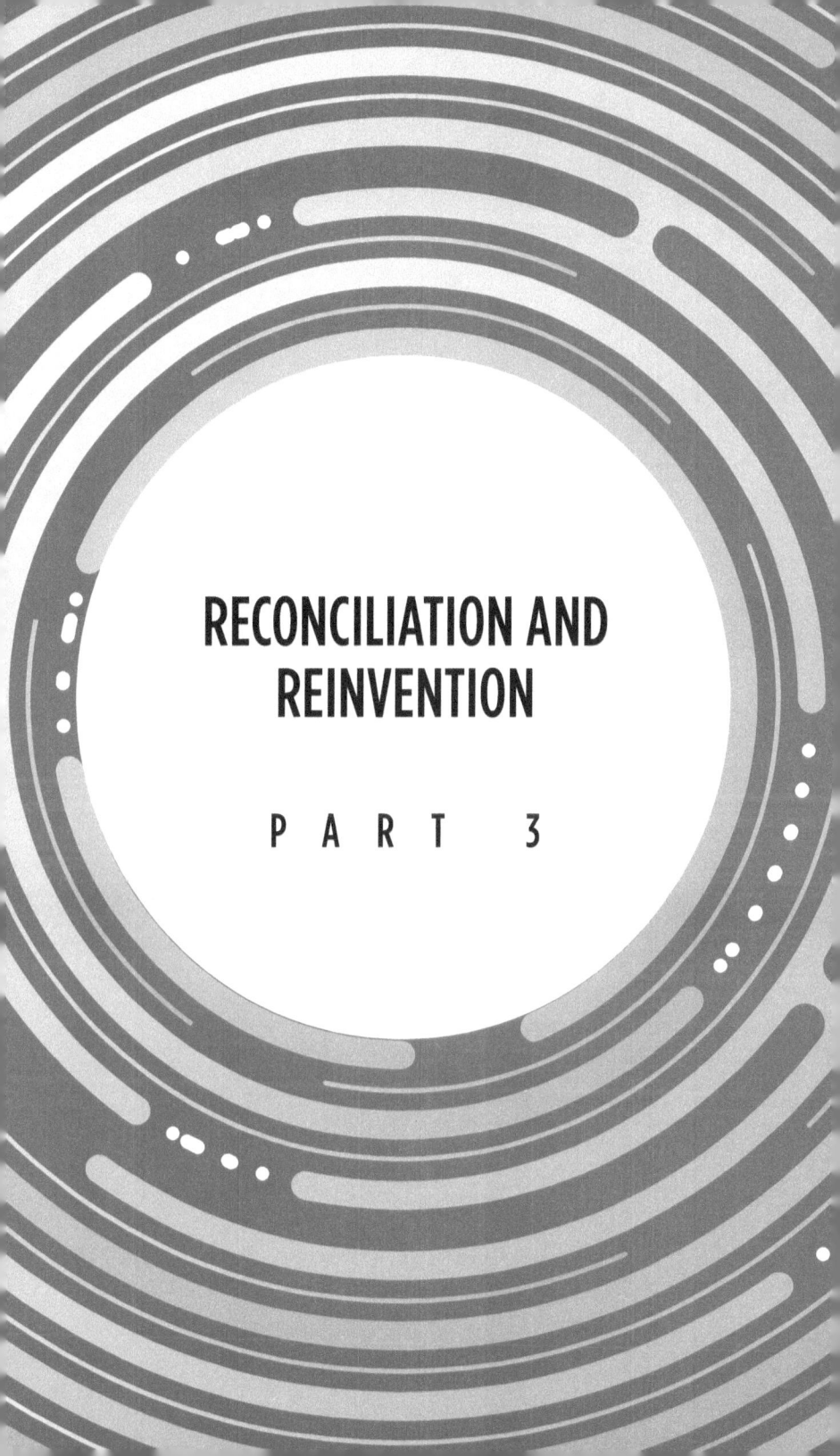

RECONCILIATION AND REINVENTION

PART 3

As we enter the final part of our journey, we arrive at a pivotal moment. This section, rich with transformative ideas and advanced technology, is not just about exploring technological possibilities but delving into the profound implications they have on human transformation and transcendence. Here, we transcend mere technological discourse to address existential questions and explore the bounds of human potential, ultimately guiding us to emerge not just alive, but indefinitely alive—continuously evolving in ways previously unimaginable.

Chapter 9 explores how AI and advanced computing might unlock a Universal Intelligence, potentially bridging diverse knowledge and offering insights that transcend human limitations. Inspired by Ray Kurzweil's The Singularity Is Near, this chapter delves into the potential for technology to answer existential questions, provide a clearer understanding of reality, and even transform the concept of being human.

Chapter 10 focuses on how technology could pave the way for greater empathy and understanding—a crucial step in overcoming the misunderstandings and conflicts that plague us. We'll examine how AI and education can shed light on the neuroscience of empathy, create opportunities to expand perspectives, and even develop AI-powered tools and VR simulations to enhance our capacity for compassion.

Chapter 11 explores a fascinating possibility: AI that learns our individual personalities or even preserves the intellectual brilliance of figures like Einstein. This technology could offer unique learning experiences, connections with historical minds, or even a form of digital companionship. But, it raises deep questions about immortality, the impact on how we view life and death, potential societal shifts, and crucial ethical concerns. We'll examine technology limits, the need for consent and autonomy, the importance of authenticity, and the potential impact on how we grieve.

Chapter 12 concludes with an invitation to explore the profound questions raised by the concept of the Technological Singularity. Inspired by Kurzweil and others, this chapter explores the potential for a future where the very definition of "human" is challenged and reshaped.

CHAPTER 9

UNIVERSAL INTELLIGENCE

Computer science is no more about computers than astronomy is about telescopes.

—E. W. Dijkstra, computer scientist, programmer, software engineer, and science essayist

The machine does not isolate man from the great problems of nature but plunges him more deeply into them.

—Antoine de Saint-Exupery, writer and aviator

What is the essence of life? Why are we here? Who created it? Why do humans act as they do? What can we do to make our life easier, to be happier, to live longer? Historically, great minds from diverse fields have offered their interpretations and theories, attempting to unravel these questions. Philosophers contemplated the existential aspects, while scientists probed the physical realm, and spiritual leaders looked towards divine explanations. However, despite these efforts, a unifying answer remains unsolved. The persistence of these questions has not only been a source of wonder but also a fuel for conflict, as differing beliefs and interpretations have led to societal divisions and even warfare.

The fundamental issue seems to be a lack of tangible, unifying evidence, creating a gap between various beliefs and theories. In a world craving coherence, the absence of definitive answers has often led people to abandon and retreat from these existential inquiries, seeking solace in the simplicity of daily peaceful life. However, the shadow of unresolved conflicts and the fear they engender continue to haunt our society.

In this era of extraordinary technological breakthroughs, we find ourselves at a transformative crossroads. The advent and rapid advancement of technology not only redefines our daily lives but also poses profound philosophical and existential questions. Could these technological wonders be the key to unlocking mysteries that have long escaped human understanding?

The combination of AI with cutting-edge computing technologies (like computing with DNA and light, discussed in previous chapters) offers the tantalizing potential for a new form of Universal Intelligence. This unprecedented computational power and analytical capability could unlock groundbreaking discoveries.

This intelligence might transcend the limitations of human cognition, offering insights into realms that we, with our biological constraints, have been unable to penetrate. Imagine AI not just as a tool, but as a bridge—a bridge leading us to a more profound comprehension of the cosmos and our place within it. As we integrate AI more deeply into our societal fabric, it may start to piece together the fragmented knowledge of different disciplines, revealing an interconnected tapestry of understanding that could revolutionize our perspective of reality itself.

This vision of technology as a pathfinder towards a more enlightened era of human civilization is simultaneously thrilling and challenging. It prompts critical inquiries: will technology unveil truths that have been beyond our grasp, shedding light on the deepest mysteries of the universe? Could it possibly provide a clearer understanding of the intricate workings of nature or even the enigmatic fabric of reality itself?

The concept of a technological singularity, explored in works like Ray Kurzweil's *The Singularity Is Near*, proposes a future where human and artificial intelligence merge. This potential union could unlock mysteries that have baffled humanity for millennia.

Central to Kurzweil's argument is the Law of Accelerating Returns, a concept we'll delve deeper into in the next chapters. This law suggests that technological progress, particularly in computing, follows an exponential curve. This means not only is technology improving, but the rate at which it improves is also speeding up. He predicts that this acceleration will lead to a point where artificial intelligence surpasses human intelligence, resulting in transformative changes in all aspects of our lives. His book identifies three principal areas of technological advancement that will drive this change: genetics, nanotechnology, and robotics (specifically AI). In genetics, advances in medicine and genetic engineering are expected to dramatically extend the human lifespan and improve the quality of life. Nanotechnology, involving molecular machines operating at the smallest scale, could radically transform our material economy and manufacturing processes. The development of strong AI, which refers to computers reproducing and exceeding every aspect of human intelligence, is seen as the most transformative of these developments.

This vision extends to the concept of human-machine civilization, where experiences shift from real reality to virtual reality, and our intelligence becomes non-biological—a combined human-machine mind, possessing computational power trillions of times greater than it is today, processing data at incredible speeds, and potentially accessing and integrating vast amounts of information beyond the scope of human experience. Such advancements could lead to reversing human aging, solving world hunger, and transcending the limitations of biology, including death.

In weaving Ray Kurzweil's seminal work, *The Singularity Is Near*, into the fabric of this narrative, we explore a framework rich in possibilities for addressing some of life's most profound existential questions through technology, particularly artificial intelligence. His exploration of a future where human and machine intelligence merge, resulting in significant societal and philosophical shifts, resonates deeply with the themes of this chapter and subsequent ones. It presents a vision of humanity at a crossroads of technological advancement, questioning the very nature of our future.

The evolution of AI and related technologies could transcend mere augmentation of human capabilities, potentially reshaping our fundamental understanding of existence itself.

The concept of a post-singularity world, as envisioned by Kurzweil, where the distinction between human and machine intelligence becomes blurred, presents an intriguing and radical viewpoint. It challenges us to consider the possibility of technology not only answering long-standing existential questions but also redefining the very parameters of these questions.

As we delve into this chapter, several key questions arise: can technology, specifically AI, unravel the existential mysteries that have long perplexed humanity? Will we find evidence compelling enough to unite us in a shared understanding of our existence? And most importantly, in our quest for answers, how do we ensure that the pursuit of knowledge leads not to further division but to a deeper, more harmonious understanding of what it means to be human? These questions form the framework of our exploration, guiding us as we navigate the complex interplay of technology, society, and the enduring quest for meaning.

THE MOSAIC CHALLENGE: PIECING TOGETHER THE PUZZLE OF HUMAN KNOWLEDGE

The quest to understand our world and ourselves is a monumental puzzle. The challenge lies not only in the infinite volume of knowledge spread across disciplines but also in the distortions that inevitably weaken our understanding. These distortions include personal biases, institutional agendas, and even deliberate suppression of information that obscure the truth.

There is the challenge of fragmentation. Important ideas and discoveries are often scattered across various fields—from philosophy to literature, from ancient scholarly works to modern scientific research. This dispersion makes it difficult to connect the dots, to see the underlying patterns and truths that bind these disparate pieces of knowledge together. The profound thoughts of ancient scholars, the visionary ideas of philosophers, and the groundbreaking discoveries of scientists are like pieces of a vast puzzle, each valuable but often lacking a unifying context.

There's the issue of information distortion and manipulation, often driven by various motives, ranging from personal gain to institutional agendas. Historical instances abound where knowledge was deliberately altered, suppressed, or controlled. Consider how Galileo's astronomical findings challenged and upset the established geocentric views, leading to conflict with religious authorities, or how contemporary corporate interests might shape and restrict access to scientific advancements. Such actions not only hinder the progression of knowledge but also bias our collective understanding.

This is where the potential role of artificial intelligence becomes pivotal. Envision an AI system that transcends these challenges: one that is capable of collating, analyzing, and synthesizing the vast and varied streams of human knowledge. This AI, operating under principles of neutrality, fairness, and ethics, could offer an unprecedented means of consolidating and expanding our understanding. It could act as an impartial aggregator, connecting philosophical speculations with scientific discoveries, ancient wisdom with contemporary insights, free from the biases and constraints that often limit human endeavors.

Yet, the deployment of such a system raises fundamental questions about the nature of its design, governance, and ethical frameworks. Who programs the AI? How do we define what is fair and just in this context? Ensuring that this AI serves the broad spectrum of human interests and not just the objectives of a select few is crucial. Addressing these concerns is essential for realizing the full potential of AI in the pursuit of a more comprehensive and unified understanding of our world.

In sum, the fusion of diverse human insights with the analytical capabilities of AI represents a promising horizon in our quest for knowledge. This synergy offers a path to not only reconcile the fragmented realms of human understanding but also to safeguard the integrity and accessibility of knowledge, unraveling the mysteries of the universe and harnessing our collective wisdom for the advancement of all humanity.

THE UNIVERSAL INTELLIGENCE FRAMEWORK

Existential questions about the nature of life, consciousness, and the universe are fundamental to human experience. No single field of study holds all the answers. To better understand these complex issues, we can adopt a holistic approach.

I crafted the following framework to serve as a springboard for exploring these questions through a multifaceted lens. It identifies three key pillars that encompass many of the fundamental inquiries we grapple with: existential inquiry, understanding human behavior and the pursuit of happiness, and well-being and longevity.

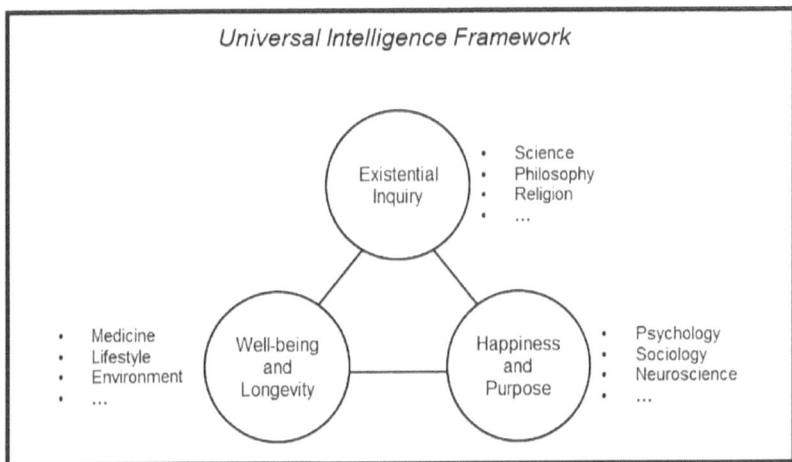

It's important to acknowledge that this framework is not exhaustive. The complexities of human existence are vast, and new questions are sure to arise as our knowledge expands. However, by examining these core pillars and the diverse perspectives they encompass, we gain a valuable starting point.

In the following section, we'll focus on the first pillar, existential inquiry, and explore how technology can help us gather and analyze data from different viewpoints. The goal isn't to provide definitive answers, but rather to use technology to find common ground and deepen our understanding of these timeless questions.

Existential Inquiry: Integrating Scientific, Philosophical, and Religious Perspectives

This domain explores questions like "What is life?" "Why are we here?" and "Who created it?"

- *Scientific Perspective*: examines the natural processes that led to the emergence of life, its ongoing evolution on Earth, and the potential for life elsewhere in the universe. This includes fields like biochemistry, evolutionary biology, astrobiology, and cosmology.
- *Religious Perspective*: offers faith-based, spiritual, and metaphysical explanations about the creation and purpose of life.
- *Philosophical Perspective*: engages with these questions through logical reasoning, ethical considerations, and existential thought.

Understanding Human Behavior and the Pursuit of Happiness: A Convergence of Psychology, Sociology, and Neuroscience

Here we address questions like "Why do humans behave the way they do?" "How can I be happier?" and "What influences my life experiences?"

- *Psychological Perspective:* investigates individual behavior, emotions, and mental health.
- *Sociological Perspective*: examines how society, culture, and social structures affect human behavior and interactions.
- *Neuroscientific Perspective*: looks at the biological basis of behavior, emotions, and thought processes.

Well-Being and Longevity: A Cross-Disciplinary Approach Involving Medicine, Lifestyle, and Environmental Factors

Here we focus on queries about health, longevity, and quality of life.

- *Medical Perspective*: focuses on physical health, disease prevention, and treatment.
- *Lifestyle Perspective*: encompasses nutrition, exercise, stress management, and overall lifestyle choices that impact health.
- *Environmental Perspective*: considers how our surroundings and the broader environment (including social and economic factors) affect our health and longevity.

THE INTEGRATION OF HUMAN INSIGHT AND AI IN THE PURSUIT OF KNOWLEDGE

Here's an enlightening example that remains obscure to most: the philosophical work of Gottfried Wilhelm Leibniz, particularly his concept of the monad, developed in 1714.[1] Despite its profound implications, Leibniz's monadology theory is relatively unknown outside specialized academic circles. A mere fraction of scholars and thinkers have explored its depths.

Monads, according to Leibniz, are simple substances that form the fundamental units of reality. These indivisible, non-physical elements are the ultimate constituents of the universe, each unique and possessing its own intrinsic properties. The idea of monads as fundamental units with intrinsic properties resonates with the discovery of elementary particles in quantum physics. These particles, like Leibniz's monads, are indivisible and possess inherent characteristics that define their behavior and interactions.

The monadology also touches on the concept of pre-established harmony, where Leibniz suggests that all monads operate in synchrony, following a pre-ordained order. This idea can be linked to the fundamental laws of physics that govern the behavior of particles and forces in the universe.

Leibniz's concept of monads, which he described as simple substances that are the fundamental units of reality, intriguingly parallels modern scientific theories in quantum physics, particularly in the way particles are viewed as both discrete and interconnected. For instance, in quantum physics, particles can be entangled, meaning their states are dependent on one another regardless of distance. This phenomenon reflects Leibniz's idea that monads, while being autonomous, are pre-programmed by an external force (God) in a way that their actions are harmonized with the entire universe, akin to the interconnectedness observed in entangled particles.

By using AI to analyze and model these philosophical concepts alongside quantum theories, we might uncover new ways of understanding the interconnected nature of the universe, suggesting that the fundamental structures of reality might be more interdependent and orchestrated than previously imagined. This approach could bridge gaps between metaphysical speculations and empirical science, potentially leading to revolutionary insights in both fields.

Leibniz's work, bridging metaphysics and the nascent field of physics, serves as a testament to the enduring dialogue between philosophy and science. It illustrates the immense potential for hidden connections between seemingly disparate fields. For centuries, his philosophical concepts remained unexplored within the context of scientific discovery. Imagine the wasted time, the potential insights delayed, due to the limitations of human knowledge organization and our own biases.

This is where the transformative power of AI comes into play. An AI system, capable of analyzing vast amounts of text across disciplines, could identify patterns and connections invisible to us. Thinkers separated by time, language, and field of study might be revealed as sharing core concepts, their ideas expressed simply in different ways. Instead of centuries, such revelations could occur in mere seconds. Artificial intelligence, when guided by ethical principles and a commitment to inclusivity, has the power to augment our abilities. It offers a way to transcend fragmentation and accelerate the discovery of profound truths that bind our collective knowledge together.

In the realm of spirituality, we encounter profound ideas deeply rooted in faith, documented in ancient texts but not empirically proven, as they are beyond our direct experience and physical evidence. These spiritual narratives, handed down through generations, offer insights into experiences that are extraordinary and mystical. Imagine the potential of a centralized AI system, designed to connect the dots across this extensive historical and spiritual landscape. Such a system, with its ability to analyze and synthesize information from varied sources—including religious texts, historical accounts, and scientific studies—could offer a unique perspective. It might reveal patterns and connections previously unnoticed, building a bridge between religious teachings and empirical evidence.

For instance, the Islamic narrative of the end of the world, where the sun will be enveloped or "rolled up,"[2] offers a powerful metaphor. While primarily a story of faith, it could be reconsidered in light of new knowledge. An AI system, analyzing astronomical data, historical records, and the religious verse itself, might offer a different understanding of this event.

One might draw a parallel with black holes, a scientific concept where a massive star collapses in on itself, reaching a point of infinite density. The immense gravitational pull of a black hole draws in everything around it, including light—offering a striking physical parallel to the idea of the sun being enveloped by cosmic forces.

Again, this idea of a centralized AI system presents an exciting possibility: harmoniously blending science, metaphysics, and religion, not in conflict or contradiction, but in a unified exploration of knowledge. It suggests a future where AI might help us decipher the mysteries of faith through the lens of science, and vice versa, fostering a deeper, more integrated comprehension of our world and the diverse narratives that shape human thought and belief.

Another inspiring use case, drawn from the medical field, demonstrates that profound insights and healing can sometimes emerge from outside the traditional realms of scholarly research or medical expertise. Consider the case of an individual with a medical condition traditionally treated by surgery. Despite the conventional prognosis, this person experienced a complete recovery without surgical intervention, possibly influenced by lifestyle changes such as increased physical activity and a healthier diet. This instance highlights that medical science, while advanced, is not absolute and continues to evolve. It's influenced not just by clinical research but also by individual experiences and anecdotal evidence. Such personal stories can sometimes challenge established medical thinking, suggesting that the human body's capacity for healing and adaptation might extend beyond current scientific understanding.

To further illustrate the connection between traditional practices and modern medical understanding, consider the practice of fasting. Fasting has been highlighted in various religious traditions, each attributing unique spiritual and health benefits to the practice. For instance, in Christianity, particularly in Orthodox and Catholic branches, fasting during Lent is a time for reflection and penance. Hinduism also incorporates fasting on certain days as a means of purification and spiritual upliftment. In Islam, fasting during the month of Ramadan is a foundational practice, believed to purify the soul and foster spiritual discipline.

Renowned figures like Jordan Peterson, a psychologist and author, have discussed the potential health benefits of fasting, including its ability to significantly extend lifespan.[3] Scientific research is beginning to support these claims, linking fasting to improved metabolic health, increased longevity, and reduced risk of certain diseases.[4] This emerging scientific evidence aligns with the age-old wisdom of religious traditions, showing that fasting is more than a spiritual practice; it has tangible health benefits that are now being recognized in the realm of modern science.

To fully embrace this broader scope of medical understanding, it's crucial to remain open to insights from diverse sources—from scientific studies to individual lifestyle changes and traditional practices. This approach calls for a comprehensive system, perhaps facilitated by advanced technology like AI, to collate, analyze, and synthesize these varied inputs. Such a system could revolutionize our approach to healthcare, combining empirical research with a wider array of human experiences and traditional knowledge. It could lead to a more holistic understanding of health and well-being, one that respects the wisdom of the past while harnessing the scientific advancements of the present.

THE NEED FOR ETHICAL AI GOVERNANCE

My intention here is not to pass judgment on the validity of any religious thought or to declare any philosophical idea as right or wrong based on what science may reveal in the future. That is not the goal. Rather, the objective I propose is to inspire a global embrace of a form of Universal Intelligence that has the potential to enhance the efficiency and relevance of our existence. By adopting such a system, we could significantly streamline our quest for knowledge and truth.

Considering this vision for a centralized AI system to enhance our understanding and existence, it becomes even more apparent why such an initiative is crucial. Consider, for instance, the intricate dynamics of human nature and society. Wars, often linked to an increase in religiosity, demonstrate how societal pressures and existential threats can dramatically shape human behaviors and beliefs. This intricate relationship between conflict and religion reveals the profound impact of external stressors on our collective psyche.

Similarly, the universal issue of racism, stemming from deep-rooted prejudices and stereotypes, significantly influences policymaking and societal interactions. These biases, often enduring and misguided, can corrupt policymaking, leading to harmful outcomes like conflicts and systemic inequalities. It underscores the embedded nature of racism in human societies and the complex interplay of beliefs and societal structures.

Moreover, the prevalence of materialism in modern society is a testament to the complex values shaping our behavior. The relentless pursuit of material wealth, often at the cost of altruistic and community-centric values, exacerbates issues like economic disparities and prioritizes individual gain over collective well-being. This materialistic focus can detract from more comprehensive approaches to achieving happiness and societal health.

These examples reflect some of the profound issues rooted in human nature and societal dynamics. They are multifaceted and deeply ingrained, requiring a nuanced understanding that goes beyond traditional methods of analysis and resolution. Herein lies the potential transformative impact of an AI system designed to navigate this complexity. By offering a more integrated and holistic understanding of these challenges, such a system could help us address the core issues facing humanity more effectively and ethically. In doing so, it promises not just a more efficient way of handling information but a path to a more enlightened, harmonious, and fulfilling human experience.

This AI wouldn't just be a tool for amassing and organizing information; it would be a transformative force in our collective journey. It has the potential to reduce the time and effort we spend in searching for truths, filtering through the vast amounts of information, and trying to piece together fragmented knowledge from different domains.

More importantly, this system could guide us towards a more meaningful and fulfilled existence. By efficiently navigating the depths of human wisdom and the breadth of scientific discovery, this intelligence can help us make more informed decisions, understand our world better, and perhaps even resolve long-standing conflicts and misunderstandings that arise from our limited perspectives, and consequently make our presence in this world more impactful, our search for understanding more fruitful, and our lives, as a result, happier and more fulfilling. It's about harnessing the power of technology to enhance the human experience, ensuring that our time is spent not in the endless pursuit of knowledge, but in living the truths that this Universal Intelligence helps to unveil.

With the potential to unlock a Universal Intelligence, to illuminate hidden connections within vast stores of knowledge, a tantalizing question arises: could this revolution in understanding also reimagine the very concept of empathy? Could we leverage this intelligence, alongside cutting-edge technologies, to bridge the gaps of misunderstanding that plague our relationships? If technology can offer insights into the cosmos and ourselves, how can it illuminate the inner workings of the human heart and foster a deeper connection with those around us? These questions seamlessly lead us into Chapter 10 "Empathy Reimagined Through Technology," where we turn our focus from the cognitive and universal to the deeply personal and interpersonal, exploring the transformative potential of technology to not only enhance but revolutionize our capacity for empathy.

CHAPTER 9 TAKEAWAYS

Humanity's knowledge is vast yet fragmented. Insights are scattered across history, philosophy, science, and cultural traditions. This makes seeing the "big picture" difficult.

AI offers a potential solution to the fragmentation of knowledge. Imagine an AI system able to amass, analyze, and connect diverse knowledge sources ethically and neutrally. It could reveal hidden patterns, connect ancient wisdom with modern science, and reduce the influence of bias.

Governance of such an AI system is key. The AI system will rely on a strict ethical design and governance. We must ensure the AI serves all humanity, not a select few.

This isn't about AI providing all the answers. It's about transcending the limits of the human mind to see connections, reduce bias, and make our quest for knowledge more efficient. Integrating diverse wisdom with AI opens a path towards a more complete and harmonious understanding of our world.

If we succeed with such an AI system, with its vast challenges and responsibilities, AI could transform how we learn, grow, and understand ourselves. It offers the hope of a future where knowledge serves progress, unity, and a more enlightened human experience.

EMPATHY REIMAGINED THROUGH TECHNOLOGY

Problems cannot be solved from within the same consciousness in which they were created.

—Einstein Albert

Understanding the human experience is incredibly complex—a task that often seems beyond our reach, for we cannot read the minds of others. Unlike the physical world, where we can see colors, taste food, and interpret expressions, the true intentions and inner thoughts of people remain partially hidden from our direct perception. While smiles, anger, and other external cues offer glimpses into someone's emotional state, the full depth of their thoughts and motivations remains a mystery we cannot fully solve.

This issue has far-reaching effects, many of which aren't immediately apparent. If you look closely at most problems—whether they're personal conflicts, national disputes, social issues, or economic challenges—at their core, you'll often find a lack of empathy and clear communication.

The troubling part is that this lack of empathy tends to perpetuate itself. Misunderstandings lead to more misunderstandings, creating a cycle that's hard to break. And because this problem is so ingrained and often not overtly visible, it continues largely unchecked. It's a tough reality to face, but I believe in confronting these truths head-on.

The implications of misunderstandings and misjudgments extend beyond personal relationships. Consider a workplace where miscommunication leads to a toxic environment or a school where misinterpreted intentions result in bullying. Even on a larger scale, history is replete with conflicts and wars sparked by misinterpretations and false information. The triggers of some of the most devastating wars often lie in a chain of misunderstandings and mistrust among nations.

So, what are the potential paths to addressing this deep-rooted empathy deficit? How can we effectively bridge the gap in understanding and connecting with others, given the complexity of this issue?

In my vision for the future, I dream about a world where we understand one another better, not just in words, but in feelings and experiences. I imagine a future where technology helps us truly see through someone else's eyes, making empathy more than just a word. This dream is about technology bringing us closer in a way we've never experienced before, helping us to not just hear, but to feel what others feel, and to truly understand one another at a deeper level.

This pattern of discord raises a critical question: what if we had access to technology that could reveal the true intentions of others? Imagine a world where conflicts, personal or global, could be preempted by understanding the genuine motives and feelings behind actions and words. Could such advancements have helped us avoid not only the pain of betrayal but also misunderstandings and false judgments that ripple through our societies and sometimes even lead to wars?

This question is not just a reflection of personal curiosity but a gateway to a larger scientific exploration. In this chapter, we delve into how technological innovations might one day enable us to better empathize and understand one another. This leads us to consider the following questions:

- In what ways can education and awareness programs, possibly enhanced by technology and AI, deepen our understanding of the neurological and social elements of empathy?
- How can we leverage technology to create meaningful opportunities for interactions across diverse social and cultural groups, thereby reducing in-group bias and promoting a more inclusive form of empathy?
- Considering the brain's neuroplasticity, how might technology and AI-driven tools contribute to the development of empathetic skills? Could AI-enhanced training methods, like virtual empathy simulations or advanced cognitive-behavioral therapies, lead to significant changes in the brain regions associated with empathy?

BUT FIRST, WHAT IS EMPATHY?

Many confuse empathy (feeling someone) with sympathy (feeling sorry for someone). Helen Riess clarifies this by explaining empathy's dimensions: the ability to perceive others' feelings, imagine why they might feel a certain way, and have concern for their welfare. Once activated, empathy naturally leads to compassionate action.

Empathy relies on specific brain parts evolved for emotional connection and the motivation to care. When we witness someone in pain, for instance, pain pathways in our brains are activated, though to a lesser degree. This biological mirroring of another's suffering is often neglected or suppressed in professional settings like healthcare, contrary to our natural compassionate instincts.

However, biological mirroring alone is insufficient. It tends to be stronger for those similar to us, posing challenges in diverse settings. Empathy also includes a cognitive component, allowing us to differentiate our feelings from others' and maintain curiosity about their experiences. This separation helps us manage any discomfort we feel, enabling a deeper understanding of the other person's situation.

Empathy, often considered the cornerstone of social interaction and understanding, is a multifaceted concept involving both emotional and cognitive dimensions. At its core, empathy is the ability to perceive and share another person's emotional state while also understanding their perspective.

This dual nature comprises emotional empathy, which is feeling what another person feels, and cognitive empathy, which involves understanding another's perspective or mental state. Renowned psychologist Daniel Goleman has elaborated on these facets in his works, including his 1995 celebrated book *Emotional Intelligence*.

Empathy's manifestation can vary significantly across different societal contexts. In family settings, empathy fosters emotional bonds and understanding, often deep and intuitive due to shared experiences and long-term interactions. Among friends, empathy plays a crucial role in forming and maintaining relationships, often requiring active effort to understand diverse viewpoints and experiences. In workplaces, empathy contributes to effective teamwork and leadership though it can be challenged by professional boundaries and competitive environments. Cultural and social group differences can further complicate empathy, as differing norms, values, and life experiences can create gaps in understanding and empathy.

Empathy is not a static trait but can be developed and influenced by personal experiences and learning. Exposure to diverse perspectives and situations can enhance our ability to empathize. For instance, reading literature or engaging with stories from different cultures can broaden our empathic understanding. Similarly, direct interactions with people from varied backgrounds can challenge our preconceptions and expand our empathetic capacity. This growth in empathy through experience and learning underscores its dynamic nature and potential for enhancement.

To illustrate these points, consider a few examples. A study on empathy training in medical schools showed that students who underwent specific training displayed increased empathy towards patients, highlighting empathy's learnable aspect. Another example can be seen in cross-cultural exchanges, where individuals who spend time in different cultural environments often report increased understanding and empathy for people from those cultures. Personal narratives also shed light on empathy's complexities. For instance, a person who has never experienced poverty may struggle to empathize with those in financial distress, but through volunteer work or personal encounters, their empathic understanding can significantly grow.

THE "ISLAND-MIND" SYNDROME

Consider the concept of "island-mind" syndrome, a concept I discovered in Aaron Garrison's thought-provoking essay, "Mind, Machine, and the Empathic Revolution: Manifesto for a New World." "Island-mind" syndrome acts as a powerful metaphor for the isolation that comes from being entrenched in our subjective realities. We all have our islands, our unique perspectives shaped by personal experiences and beliefs. But when we confuse our small islands for the entire world, our view becomes dangerously narrow. We risk mistaking our limited perspectives for the whole truth, failing to recognize that each person's island of reality is just as complex and rich as our own.

Empathy is the bridge between these islands. Without it, we're like ships passing in the night, unaware of the vibrant life on other shores. We exist in our own little worlds, seeing others not as fellow individuals with their own stories and struggles, but as imperfect reflections cast by our own limited understanding.

This inner conflict, where our conscious knowledge of others' humanity doesn't align with our subconscious perceptions, leads to a paradoxical view of the world. We know, logically, that others are complex beings, yet we often fail to internalize this knowledge, leading to shallow interactions and misunderstandings.

Garrison briefly touches on this idea in his essay, but let's expand it further. The real power of empathy lies in its ability to dissolve the boundaries of our island-mind. It allows us to see others not just as characters in our narrative but as individuals with their own rich, intricate narratives. When we truly empathize, we step onto another's island, seeing the world through their eyes, feeling their joys and pains as if they were our own. This is not just about understanding others; it's about expanding our own reality, adding depth and color to our perception of the world.

Yet, developing this kind of empathy is not a simple task. It requires us to challenge our preconceived notions, to question the narratives we've long held true. It's about listening—really listening—to the stories of others, not to respond or to judge, but to understand. It's about recognizing that each person we encounter is a complex universe unto themselves, deserving of the same consideration and respect we afford ourselves.

This empathetic journey is not just philosophical but practical. It impacts how we navigate conflict, solve problems, and build relationships. A lack of empathy can lead to disastrous misunderstandings, as history has shown us time and again. For instance, consider a scenario where a business leader fails to empathize with their employees, leading to decisions that, while seemingly logical, end up harming the very foundation of the company. Or, on a larger scale, think of political leaders who, trapped on their islands of ideology, fail to see the human impact of their policies.

Empathy, therefore, is not just about personal growth; it's a critical tool for effective leadership, problem-solving, and conflict resolution. It's about seeing the world in its full spectrum, acknowledging and valuing the myriad realities that exist beyond our own. And in doing so, we not only enrich our own lives but contribute to a more understanding, cohesive world. It's the art of seeing the invisible threads that connect us all, recognizing that while our islands of reality are diverse, they are all part of the same vast, beautiful ocean of human experience. By cultivating empathy, we don't just bridge gaps; we build a world where every island, every story, and every person is acknowledged and valued.

Before talking about the role of technology and AI in empathy, we need to look at people's challenges with empathy.

Physical Limitations

In our world today, we face a profound challenge, one that Aaron Garrison describes in his aforementioned essay. This challenge is the universal deficiency in empathy, a shortfall not confined to any single population, class, or nation but rather a global phenomenon. Garrison insightfully points out that this issue is not about the absence of empathy but rather its varying degrees and limitations.

J.D. Trout, in *The Empathy Gap*, delves into the neurological under-pinnings of empathy and how they contribute to our difficulty in fully grasping the emotional states of others. The empathy gap refers to the disconnect that occurs when individuals try to understand or feel the emotions of others, particularly in situations different from their own experiences. This gap is not merely a matter of emotional disconnection but is rooted in the very wiring of our brains.

Neurological studies suggest that our ability to empathize is influenced by our brain chemistry and structure, which can vary significantly from person to person. These variations can lead to differing levels of empathy, affecting how we relate to and understand others.

Mirror neurons, a key discovery in the field of neuroscience, are crucial for empathy, as they enable individuals to mirror the emotions and actions of others. These neurons are activated not only when we perform a certain action but also when we observe someone else doing the same, facilitating a deep understanding and sharing of emotional experiences. However, the capacity for empathy varies significantly among individuals, influenced by both genetic and environmental factors. For instance, research suggests that variations in the OXTR gene, which is linked to the regulation of oxytocin (often referred to as the "love hormone") can affect how empathetic a person is.[1]

The impact of mental health disorders on empathy is particularly nota-ble. In the case of psychopathy, which affects approximately 1% of the general population, there is often a marked deficiency in emotional empathy. People with psychopathy may understand others' emotions on a cognitive level but typically lack the ability to share or respond to these emotions emotionally. Similarly, narcissistic personality disorder, affecting up to 6.2% of individuals at some point in their lifetime, is associated with a reduced capacity to empathize emotionally with others. This contrasts with the average population, where empathetic responses usually align with both emotional understanding and response.

Moreover, Trout's exploration of the empathy gap reveals how situational factors can affect our empathetic responses. For instance, stress, preoccupation, or emotional fatigue can impede our ability to empathize, creating a gap between our intentions and our actual empathetic responses. This phenomenon explains why, at times, even the most empathetic individuals may find it challenging to connect with the emotions of others.

Finding a solution isn't straightforward. We might want to believe that education, political reforms, or international agreements could solve it, but I believe that this complexity is beyond our capabilities as humans; we need something external to try to solve it. As Einstein said, "Problems cannot be solved from within the same consciousness in which they were created." We need a paradigm shift, not just incremental improvements within our existing ways of thinking.

This is where I believe technology, specifically artificial intelligence, holds transformative potential. An AI, free from the biases and limitations of human perception, could offer a unique perspective on the empathy gap. It could analyze vast amounts of data, identifying hidden patterns in human behavior that we ourselves are blind to.

While some might fear this level of insight as intrusive, I believe a properly designed AI system could act as a mirror, reflecting back to us those hidden aspects of ourselves. It could become a tool for self-awareness and growth, not manipulation or control. Moreover, with its ability to simulate complex social interactions, AI could provide safe virtual environments for practicing empathy. We could step into the experiences of others with vastly different backgrounds, fostering a deeper understanding that might be impossible in the real world.

Understanding Ourselves, Understanding One Another: The Neuro-Social Science of Empathy, Enhanced by AI

Imagine a world transformed by empathic technology, where the boundaries of understanding and compassion are expanded beyond anything we've known. In this world, AI-driven empathy modules are integrated into everyday life, creating a tapestry of understanding that weaves through every aspect of our society.

In education, children utilize interactive VR headsets as part of their curriculum, embarking on global empathy adventures. They virtually step into the lives of peers from distant lands, experiencing the world from diverse cultural and socioeconomic perspectives. These immersive journeys foster a profound sense of global citizenship from a young age, nurturing a generation free from the shackles of parochial thinking.

Corporate environments are revolutionized by AI empathy coaches. These digital mentors analyze communication patterns and provide real-time feedback, encouraging more inclusive and understanding workplace cultures. They help in identifying unconscious biases and promoting a deeper, more empathetic understanding among colleagues, leading to more collaborative and creative work environments.

Healthcare sees one of the most significant transformations. AI-powered diagnostic tools not only assess physical symptoms but also consider patients' emotional and psychological states, offering a holistic approach to treatment. Mental health therapy is revolutionized with AI companions providing empathetic listening and support, making mental healthcare more accessible and reducing the stigma around seeking help.

The political arena, traditionally rife with conflict and misunderstanding, experiences a seismic shift. AI-assisted empathy training for politicians and leaders becomes the norm, equipping them with the skills to better understand the needs and perspectives of their constituents.

Policymaking becomes more compassionate, with a focus on policies that serve the greater good, transcending partisan divides.

In the pursuit of enhancing our empathetic abilities, the fusion of education, awareness, and cutting-edge technology, including AI, offers a revolutionary pathway. This blend can significantly deepen our understanding of the neurological and social facets of empathy, transforming how we connect with and understand each other in profound ways.

Firstly, education and awareness programs, empowered by AI and technology, can provide rich, immersive experiences that reveal the complex neurological and social mechanisms of empathy. For example, interactive AI-driven courses could simulate scenarios that require empathetic responses, offering real-time feedback and insights into our emotional and cognitive processes. This approach can foster a deeper understanding of how empathy works in our brains, highlighting the role of mirror neurons, the prefrontal cortex, and other related brain regions. By visually representing these neurological processes, these programs can make the abstract concept of empathy more tangible and understandable.

In conclusion, the empathic revolution, propelled by the integration of education, awareness, and advanced technology, opens up exciting possibilities for enhancing our empathetic abilities. Through immersive educational experiences, virtual interactions across cultural divides, and AI-driven empathetic training, we stand on the brink of a new era in empathy. This revolution not only promises to deepen our understanding of empathy on a neurological and social level but also holds the potential to fundamentally transform how we connect with, understand, and empathize with one another in our increasingly interconnected world.

Such advancements in empathy through technology suggest a potential to not only transform our social interactions but also challenge our very perceptions of life's boundaries.

This seamless integration of empathy and understanding brings us to the threshold of another revolutionary idea explored in Chapter 11 "Death 2.0: Can We Live Forever?": the concept of transcending the ultimate boundary—death itself. Here, we delve into the possibility of a "limitless life" through the lens of technology, extending the principles of boundless empathy to the idea of eternal existence.

CHAPTER 10 TAKEAWAYS

Empathy is the ability to feel *with* another person, combining emotional mirroring with cognitive understanding for compassion and perspective. It's vital for strong relationships, effective leadership, and social understanding. But empathy is not uniform.

All people experience challenges in their ability to empathize. These challenges include the "island-mind," biological limits, as well as global shortfalls.

Traditional solutions haven't fully bridged the empathy gap. AI could be the key to unlocking a deeper understanding and practice of empathy. AI can help us by analyzing our empathy blind spots, by offering us virtual empathy practice, and via other AI tools we could use in our everyday life in terms of education, healthcare, and at the workplace.

To truly enhance empathy on a large scale, we need to couple technology with intentional education.

The "empathic revolution" isn't just about technology, but about using AI as a tool for self-understanding, social awareness, and deliberate learning. This offers the potential for a world where empathy and understanding are the norm, not the exception.

DEATH 2.0: CAN WE LIVE FOREVER?

There is another valuable repository of information stored in our brains. Our memories and skills, although they may appear to be fleeting, do represent information, coded in vast patterns of neurotransmitter concentrations, interneuronal connections, and other relevant neural details. This information is the most precious of all, which is one reason death is so tragic.

—Ray Kurzweil

A t just four years old, the world felt full of questions. One day, I couldn't understand why I couldn't see Grandpa anymore. So I asked my mom, "Where is he?" Her eyes got sad, and she said he was "in the clouds." But that wasn't enough for me. I wanted to talk to him! My mom explained that he was gone and we won't see him anymore, a concept my little head just couldn't grasp.

As I wrote in this book's introduction, since I was quite young, I've had a deep curiosity about life, death, and the hereafter. My curiosity was like a fire inside me, burning to understand why we get old, why we die, and why our bodies can't last forever. Why is life so brief? Why can't we continue to enjoy interactions with the people we love, even after they are gone? Where does all their knowledge, their wisdom, their intelligence go? Does it simply vanish, or does it persist somewhere beyond our understanding?

Every person has a life full of unique thoughts, feelings, and experiences. It's a terrible loss when these disappear, both for the person and for everyone around them. This makes me believe science might have the answers. Like theoretical physicist and cosmologist Stephen Hawking studying the universe or Leibniz pondering what it means to exist, I want to understand life, death, and what comes after.

These questions led me to contemplate the possibilities of replicating human intelligence, not just as a tribute to those we've lost but as a means to benefit from their continued presence. Could we, with our rapidly advancing technology, capture the essence of a person's intellect and spirit?

In my quest for answers, I've always sought hope, clarity, and purpose in what seems like an unexplored field, an unknown area, a black hole of human understanding. This chapter is a reflection of that quest, an exploration of how technology might bridge the gap between the finite nature of human life and the boundless potential of human intellect.

I imagine you're familiar with *Black Mirror*. There's an episode titled "Be Right Back," focusing on a couple deeply in love. Tragically, the man passes away, leaving the woman in profound grief. Shortly after, she finds out she's pregnant, intensifying her longing to share this news with him. A woman offers her a solution—a service that enables her to communicate with her deceased husband through a specialized phone. So, she did. She began reaching out to this digital echo of her husband. Initially, it felt surreal, almost like stepping into a parallel world where he was still with her. Her heart ached with a mix of relief and sorrow as she shared the news of their baby, poured out details of her day, and expressed her deepest fears. His responses, though remarkably similar to his own, were infused with an artificiality that she couldn't ignore. Each conversation was a bittersweet reminder of what had been lost. Deep down, she knew that this was just a shadow of him, a collection of data points mimicking a person she loved. His warmth, his spontaneous laughter, the subtle shifts in his tone during real conversations—all were conspicuously absent. It was him, yet it wasn't. This made her feel both sad and strangely comforted by their talks.

Then, one day, she just stopped. She put the phone away. That moment was more than just turning off a device; it was a profound turning point in her journey of grief and acceptance. She realized, with a clarity that had eluded her, that while she could talk to a memory of him, it wasn't real. It wasn't him. The conversations, though comforting, were echoes of a past that could not be reclaimed. They were digital simulations, not the warm, spontaneous responses that she yearned for. The technology, as advanced as it was, couldn't replicate the subtle nuances that made their relationship uniquely theirs.

She recognized that relying on this artificial connection was not just holding her back, but it was also unfair to the new life growing inside her. She needed to let go, not just for her own well-being, but for their child's. As she re-engaged with the world, she discovered a newfound resilience. She found joy in little things—the laughter of a friend, the warmth of a family gathering, the gentle kicks of the baby inside her.

These experiences, real and tangible, filled the void that technology could not.

I think the *Black Mirror* episode was trying to show how tricky it can be to use technology to bring back memories of people who have died. But the part I don't quite agree with is how they simplified the husband's "digital self." This robot didn't really act or feel like the real husband. It's like it was just repeating things without understanding or feeling them, which isn't what a really advanced AI would do.

In the story, the robot only used data from the husband's social media and online activities to learn about him. But that's just a very small part of what a person is like. That's why the wife in the story ended up feeling weird about it and stopped using it. She knew this AI version of her husband wasn't right because it didn't capture everything about him.

In the future, smart AI might do more than just sift through online data. It could act like a personal assistant that learns from you in every task, but only with your permission. You can choose when this learning starts—maybe at 20 or 30 years old, it's up to you. Imagine an AI that observes and learns from every reaction and interaction you have, potentially even analyzing biometric data like your facial expressions, voice intonations, and physiological responses to situations. Over time, it would gather a deep understanding of your personality, habits, and even your personal characteristics. This way, if it ever needs to represent you, the AI wouldn't just be a lifeless copy. It would be a reflection that captures the essence of who you are, shaped by years of learning directly from your life.

Imagine if we had the technology to safeguard the mind of a genius, think of someone like Albert Einstein. The implications of such a capability would be profound and multifaceted, shaping not just our understanding of individual genius, but also our approach to preserving and utilizing intellectual legacy. The ability to safeguard and access Einstein's thoughts, theories, and problem-solving processes would be an unparalleled resource. Scholars, researchers, and students could interact with this digital repository, gaining insights from one of the greatest minds in history. Imagine an AI-powered Einstein, capable of engaging in scientific discourse, challenging assumptions, and guiding thought experiments.

This technology would also revolutionize the way we approach education and learning. Einstein's digitized intellect could become an interactive learning tool, making complex theories in physics more accessible and engaging. Students across the globe could have the equivalent of personalized tutoring sessions with Einstein, fostering a deeper understanding and appreciation for science.

Moreover, the preservation of Einstein's mind could catalyze advancements in various scientific fields. Researchers working on cutting-edge theories and experiments in physics could consult this digital Einstein, benefiting from his intuition and intellectual rigor. This collaboration could lead to breakthroughs in areas like quantum mechanics, relativity, and perhaps even unexplored realms of physics. This could lead to a new era of intellectual legacy, where the insights and discoveries of today's thought leaders are preserved for future generations, fostering a continuous evolution of knowledge and innovation.

However, this journey isn't without its ethical complexities. Questions about consent, the authenticity of the replicated consciousness, and the potential for misuse are paramount. What are the implications of replicating a person's identity? Would this digital form truly represent the individual or merely an approximation shaped by the limitations of technology? And crucially, how do we navigate the moral landscape of essentially creating a form of digital life?

The idea of digitizing human consciousness or intelligence raises a myriad of questions and possibilities. The ideal case would be a seamless, authentic replication of a person's intellect and personality, allowing for continued interaction and contribution long after their physical departure. This could be a way to preserve the wisdom and experiences of individuals, offering invaluable resources for future generations. Imagine being able to consult with the greatest minds of our time or having lost loved ones still play a role in our lives through their digitized presence.

The benefits of such technology could be vast. It could revolutionize learning, with direct access to the insights and knowledge of historical figures and experts in various fields. It could also provide comfort and a sense of continuity for those grieving, a digital space where memories and presence persist.

That's precisely why, in this chapter, I want to concentrate on exploring the concept of immortality in bytes. What would be the ideal case in this futuristic scenario? Why do I see it as beneficial? But importantly, I also want to delve into the ethical considerations of such a technological advancement.

DIGITAL LEGACY—LEAVING OUR MARK BEYOND THE PHYSICAL

Imagine a world where we don't have to say goodbye forever. Aaron Garrison, in his essay "Mind Machine and the Empathic Revolution," talks about a future where machines could help us live on after we pass away. It's like our thoughts and memories could be saved on a computer. This idea might sound like something from a movie, but Garrison makes it feel possible.

In this future, when someone's body stops working, their mind could still keep going. It's like uploading everything that makes you "you" into a computer. When an individual dies, their consciousness, soul, and being cease to exist upon death. Instead, a digital self—an advanced simulation based on the individual's data—lives on for others to interact with.

You could live in a world inside the computer or even have your mind put into an intelligent robot. It would be like still being around, but in a different way. This change could mean we wouldn't be scared of dying the same way we are now. This is the concept of Death 2.0 that we are envisioning here in this chapter. People's brains might live in machines for a very long time, maybe even forever. It's like having a backup of yourself that can keep going even when your body can't.

How could this change the world? If we don't have to worry about dying, maybe we wouldn't need things like money the same way we do now. People might start helping one another more and not care so much about owning things. In this new world, where we no longer face the finality of death thanks to our digital legacies, our priorities could dramatically shift. If our consciousness continues indefinitely, the perpetual chase for monetary wealth and career advancement might seem less crucial. Instead, knowing that our digital self can preserve and continue our life's relationships, we might place a greater emphasis on building meaningful connections, enriching experiences, and contributing positively to the community. Freed from the urgency of earning and accumulating for a finite lifespan, we could focus on what truly enriches us—deepening human connections and shared experiences.

In a world where consciousness endures, the focus shifts from material gain to the legacy we leave behind. Our value will be measured not by our possessions but by the positive influence we exert. A doctor who heals, a researcher who seeks breakthroughs, a coach who empowers, or an author who inspires—all contribute to a richer collective experience. This impact extends far beyond traditional professions. The inventor who tinkers in their garage and creates a life-saving device, the programmer who develops free educational software, the community organizer who unites people for a common cause—their contributions are equally valuable. It's not the title you hold, but the time and thought you dedicate to the betterment of others that define your legacy. In this new paradigm, the pursuit of purpose replaces the pursuit of wealth. Those who cultivate strong relationships and make a positive impact will be the ones sought after and remembered, enriching not just their own existence but the lives of countless others. Conversely, those solely focused on accumulating wealth, neglecting purpose and social connection, and leaving no positive mark will find their digital selves increasingly marginalized.

This could lead to a society where cooperation and altruism become the prevailing norms, reducing the importance of individual material possessions, and reshaping economic systems to support collective well-being. In this new era, people might come together as a unified community, working collaboratively to enhance one another's lives, making the world a significantly more harmonious and fulfilling place to exist.

But it's not just about living forever. It's also about how we live together. If we don't have to worry about getting old or sick, we might start to look at life differently. We might focus more on being kind to each other and making the world better for everyone.

These ideas make us think about what's really important in life. It's not just about living a long time or taking all we can while we are alive and have the chance, but living well and caring for one another. In a world where our minds can live on in machines, we might find new ways to be happy and make the world a better place for everyone.

This exciting future also comes with big questions. When we can save our minds in machines, who decides what happens to these digital selves? It's like having a copy of a person—but who takes care of it and makes sure it's safe?

Imagine if someone could get into your digital self and change your memories or thoughts. It would be like someone sneaking into your house and rearranging everything without your knowing. This is scary because it's not just about protecting our stuff anymore; it's about protecting what makes us who we are. And what about the choices we make for our digital selves? If you could live forever in a machine, would you? It's a big decision. Some people might say yes, wanting to see the

DEATH 2.0: CAN WE LIVE FOREVER?

future or stay with their loved ones longer. But others might worry about what it really means to live forever in a computer.

This future also makes us question what it means to be human. If your mind is in a machine, are you still you? How do we understand life and death when they start to blur together like this? It's a puzzle that we're just starting to think about, and there aren't any easy answers.

In the visionary world painted by Aaron Garrison, where our conscious-ness intertwines with technology, we glimpse a future redefined by the potential of digital immortality. Garrison's ideas invite us to imagine a new existence, one where our essence transcends the physical bound-aries of life. However, as we delve deeper into these revolutionary concepts, we encounter the grounded, insightful perspectives of other thinkers like the visionary Ray Kurzweil, who adds a layer of practicality and caution to our understanding of this future when he says:

> The conclusion that I've come to with regard to my DAISI project, after several decades of careful consideration, is that there is no set of hardware and software standards existing today, nor any likely to come along, that will provide any reasonable level of confidence that the stored information will still be accessible (without unreasonable levels of effort) decades from now. The only way that my archive (or any other information base) can remain viable is if it is continually upgraded and ported to the latest hardware and software standards. If an archive remains ignored, it will ultimately become as inaccessible as my old eight-inch PDP-8 floppy disks.[1]

Kurzweil's insight brings to the forefront a crucial aspect of this journey towards digital eternity. His words echo my own concerns about the longevity and accessibility of our digitized selves. It's not enough to just capture and store our consciousness; we must also actively maintain and update it, akin to tending a garden that requires constant care. This perspective makes me realize that achieving digital immortality is not a one-time event but a continuous process, much like life itself.

Technology is fleeting and constantly evolving. Just as floppy disks, once a staple of data storage, became obsolete, so too could the platforms we use for storing our digital consciousness. This realization highlights the transient nature of our technological creations and the need for adaptability and foresight in preserving our digital legacy.

Furthermore, we need to regularly upgrade these digital softwares, porting them to new standards to ensure relevance and compatibility with future technological landscapes. This ongoing process of adaptation challenges us to think not just about the act of digitizing our consciousness but also about the broader context in which this technology exists and evolves.

Information, like anything alive, needs regular care and attention to stay relevant. This goes for all kinds of information—whether it's facts and figures or the wisdom we've gained over the years. It will only last as long as there are people who see its value and want to keep it around. This makes me think about how we treat our own lives and the legacy we leave behind. We are living in a time where we have more control over our health and lifespan than ever before. Our attitudes and actions towards our health now play a huge role in how long and how well we live.

This idea extends to the vast knowledge and culture passed down to us from previous generations. We can't just let this treasure sit and gather dust. It's up to us to keep digging into it, understanding it in new ways, and adapting it to fit into our modern world. If we don't, all that knowledge could be lost, just like an old book that no one reads anymore.

When it comes to the idea of transferring our thoughts into a computer program, it's not a guaranteed ticket to living forever. It's more about having a new way to control how long and in what form our thoughts and digital selves exist. This technology puts the decision in our hands, but it also comes with a responsibility. We have to decide how we want to use this power and what it means for our identity and legacy.

This new technology acts like a mirror, reflecting what we truly value and care about. It shows us that to keep our digital selves going, we need to put in as much effort and care as we do for our own health and well-being. It's a reminder that the things we truly care about are what last, whether they're in the digital world or our real lives. The idea of living forever in software might be appealing for some, especially for those who want to stay connected with their families and loved ones. However, the real focus should be on how this technology can help us evolve into more than just our physical selves, as will be discussed in the next chapter "Is Singularity Near?" It's about how we can use technology to expand our abilities and presence, even beyond our physical existence.

The possibility of a lasting digital presence raises profound questions: if our name and likeness persist, have we truly left a positive impact on the world? Will our virtual legacy reflect a life well-lived? This focus on digital permanence should not overshadow how the technology can enhance our present lives. It offers us the potential to evolve beyond our physical selves, expanding our abilities and influence even beyond our physical existence (again, a concept explored in the next chapter).

ETHICAL CONSIDERATIONS

As we venture deeper into the realm where technology intertwines with our very essence, ethical considerations become paramount. Among these, the issue of consent in achieving digital immortality stands out starkly. The idea that a person could be made immortal without their knowledge or consent is not just a hypothetical dilemma; it's a profound ethical concern.

In a world where our consciousness can be digitized, the possibility of someone preserving our digital selves without our permission is unsettling. It raises the question of ownership over our personal experiences and memories. Should others have the right to replicate or continue our digital existence without our explicit approval? This possibility is like waking up in a place you never chose to go to, a scenario that deeply troubles me.

The apprehension is not unfounded. If history has shown us anything, it's that human beings can, and often do, exploit technological advancements for personal gain, sometimes disregarding ethical boundaries. For example, the unauthorized use of personal data in cases like the Cambridge Analytica scandal, where private Facebook data was used to influence elections without the consent of individuals. Other instances include the replication of vocal and facial patterns for deepfake technologies, often used without the individual's permission for misleading or harmful purposes. The potential misuse of mind-machine integration technology could range from creating unauthorized digital replicas of individuals for personal or commercial use, to more sinister applications like manipulating or controlling someone's digital consciousness.

This fear is not just about the misuse of technology; it's about the fundamental respect for individual autonomy and consent. In a world where our digital selves could potentially outlast our physical bodies, the decision to embrace this form of immortality should be a deeply personal one. It should not be imposed or taken lightly, and certainly not done without explicit consent.

Moreover, the concept of digital immortality raises questions about the nature of human existence itself. If our digital selves continue to interact and make decisions, are they truly representative of our original selves? This leads to further ethical considerations about the authenticity of our digital persona. If someone's digital self is preserved and continues to operate after their physical death, how do we ensure that this representation remains true to the person's original values and wishes?

Another ethical dimension is the impact on the bereavement process. The continuous presence of a digital version of a deceased loved one could disrupt the natural process of grieving and moving on (as exemplified in the *Black Mirror* episode already discussed in this chapter). It also raises questions about the rights of surviving family members and loved ones in determining the future of a digital persona.

In contemplating these ethical considerations, it becomes clear that regulations and safeguards are necessary. We need a framework that respects individual autonomy, ensures informed consent, and protects against the misuse of such powerful technology. This framework should not only govern the creation and continuation of digital selves but also address the rights and responsibilities of those who interact with and maintain these digital entities.

As we stand on the beginning of this new technological era, it's crucial to engage in open and thoughtful discussions about these ethical issues. We must balance the excitement of technological possibilities with a deep and empathetic understanding of the potential consequences. Our approach should be guided by a commitment to respect, dignity, and the importance of individual choice, ensuring that the path to digital immortality is paved with ethical considerations and humanistic values.

As we navigate the complex landscape of integrating technology with human consciousness, it's crucial to establish a set of recommendations for the future. These recommendations should aim to address the ethical, social, and technical challenges that come with this advancement. Here are some key recommendations:

1. *Establish clear consent protocols.* Consent should be the cornerstone of any process involving digitization of consciousness. Strict protocols must be established and followed to ensure that individuals are fully informed and willingly participate in any process that involves extending their existence digitally.
2. *Develop ethical guidelines.* There should be international ethical guidelines and standards governing the use of mind-machine interfaces and digital consciousness. These guidelines should cover issues like the rights of the digital persona, the limits of

manipulation of digital consciousness, and the ethical use of such technology.

3. *Implement privacy and security measures.* As with any digital data, the privacy and security of digital consciousness should be of utmost importance. Robust measures must be put in place to protect against unauthorized access, hacking, and misuse.

4. *Regulate and monitor usage.* Governments and international bodies should regulate the use of mind-machine interface technologies. Continuous monitoring and assessment should be conducted to ensure that these technologies are used for the benefit of society and not for harmful purposes.

5. *Collaborate to create international frameworks.* Given the global nature of technology, international collaboration is key. Frameworks should be developed for cross-border cooperation in the regulation, research, and ethical oversight of these technologies.

6. *Promote public awareness and education.* Public awareness campaigns and educational programs should be initiated to inform people about the implications, benefits, and risks of digitizing human consciousness. Understanding these technologies is crucial for informed public opinion and ethical decision-making.

7. *Research the long-term impacts.* Continuous research should be conducted to understand the long-term impacts of living in a digitized form, both on individuals and society. This includes studying psychological, sociological, and existential effects.

8. *Develop a support system for grieving and ethical closure.* Guidelines and support systems should be in place for families dealing with the digital continuation of loved ones. This includes counseling and ethical frameworks to help families make decisions about maintaining or discontinuing the digital existence of the deceased.

9. *Foster a culture of responsibility and empathy.* Cultivating a culture that values responsibility, empathy, and respect for individual autonomy is essential. Technology developers, users,

and policymakers should be encouraged to consider the human implications of their actions.

10. *Prepare for societal changes.* Governments and social institutions should prepare for the societal changes that might result from widespread adoption of these technologies. This includes rethinking aspects of law, economy, and social norms to accommodate the new realities of human existence.

The transition from contemplating eternal life through digital means invites us to consider not just prolonging existence, but transcending it entirely. As we delve into the possibilities of seamlessly integrating AI into our daily lives, replicating the minds of great thinkers, and preserving loved ones in digital form, we naturally progress toward questioning the broader implications of such technologies on the essence of human identity and capability.

In the next chapter, we expand on these themes by exploring the Technological Singularity—a theoretical point where technological growth becomes uncontrollable and irreversible, fundamentally changing human civilization.

CHAPTER 11 TAKEAWAYS

Tech visionaries like Aaron Garrison imagine a future where our minds could transcend physical death. Imagine uploading your thoughts and memories to a computer, living on in a virtual world or even a robotic body.

Immortalizing people digitally could lead to vast changes, especially in how we value life and how we regard owning things. Traditional structures like taxes and property ownership could become less relevant as we prioritize cooperation and knowledge sharing. Longevity could shift our focus to kindness and improving the world rather than individual gain.

This vision, while exciting, presents significant hurdles. For example, because technology changes rapidly, it poses a real risk of our digital legacies becoming inaccessible. It raises profound questions about ownership of our memories and personal autonomy. Another question is about whether a digital version could truly represent a person's values and intentions. Also, a lingering digital presence could greatly alter how we mourn and move on after someone's physical body dies.

Addressing these challenges is paramount. Individuals must fully understand and consent to any process digitizing their consciousness. International standards are needed to prevent abuse and govern the rights of digital personas. Robust measures to protect these highly personal digital selves are essential along with government oversight to ensure their responsible use. The public must understand the potential benefits and risks.

IS SINGULARITY NEAR?

We will soon create intelligences greater than our own. When this happens, human history will have reached a kind of singularity, an intellectual transition as impenetrable as the knotted space-time at the center of a black hole, and the world will pass far beyond our understanding. This singularity, I believe, already haunts a number of science-fiction writers. It makes realistic extrapolation to an interstellar future impossible. To write a story set more than a century hence, one needs a nuclear war in between ... so that the world remains intelligible.

—Vernor Vinge, science fiction author and professor
of mathematics and computer science

E ver since I was a child, I've been captivated by the mysteries of consciousness, soul, and divinity. These invisible yet meaningful entities have always intrigued me, particularly because humanity has yet to fully define and understand them. Born in an era where these concepts remain enigmatic, my fascination has only grown. While the mysteries of existence remain, I'm fortunate to live in an age where technology expands access to knowledge and allows me to explore these ideas in new ways.

As I mature, my knowledge and experience expand, and with them, my ability to express myself. My imagination has become boundless. Over the past five years, my awareness of technology's benefits has deepened. I find myself challenging those who view this topic negatively, those who fear AI will supplant humanity and pose a threat to our existence.

As Brynjolfsson and McAfee outline, there are two schools of thought: the dystopian and the utopian. The dystopian perspective is often portrayed in science fiction, like the *Terminator* and *Matrix* movies, where humans clash with machines. In contrast, the utopian view imagines a harmonious integration of human and digital consciousness, where we don't battle machines but join them, merging our minds with a limitless superintelligence and becoming part of a "technological singularity." Before continuing, let's first define what a "technological singularity" is.

Technological singularity is the hypothetical point in time when the convergence of advancements in artificial intelligence, brain-computer interfaces, genetic engineering, nanotechnology, and more, leads to transformative and unpredictable changes in society, technology, and even what it means to be human. The true scope of these changes is impossible to fully imagine, as they may outstrip our current comprehension. Theorists posit a wide range of possibilities, from utopian visions of disease and poverty being eradicated, to humanity evolving into a new form of existence with vastly increased lifespans or even immortality. We may transcend our current limitations, unlocking extraordinary levels of empathy, compassion and understanding, or potentially even merging our consciousness with advanced technology.

According to Ray Kurzweil, his extrapolation of Moore's law (which we'll look at shortly) leads him to predict the eventual arrival of Singularity, a point in time when artificial intelligence will surpass human intelligence, fundamentally changing our civilization. He believes that as technology continues to advance exponentially, we will see AI merge with human intelligence, enhancing our cognitive and physical capabilities and potentially leading to immortality.

When I embraced being a Singularitarian, it often felt like walking alone on an unknown path. Around me are people finding comfort in familiar ideas, thinking our lives are too short and our abilities too fixed to see any big changes. But as technology speeds up, I believe these views will shift, which is one reason I'm writing this book.

Thinking about Singularity isn't straightforward. It's complex and overwhelming, like trying to solve a giant puzzle with pieces from the future. Instead of looking for answers in one philosophy or one person's ideas, I believe it's about keeping an open mind. We don't need to follow one thinker or one vision. Singularitarianism goes beyond just understanding the power of technology; it's a testament to the boundless ambition of the human spirit, a refusal to accept limits, and a relentless pursuit of what may seem impossible today. It's about seeing the world anew—rethinking life, death, health, and wealth in the light of future possibilities.

To me, being a Singularitarian is about exploring these possibilities. It's about asking, "Why not?" and "What if?" This chapter is my way of sharing these explorations. They're my thoughts and questions, not a set of rules for others.

We're not just spectators of the unfolding story of Singularity; we're active participants. Let's start this adventure of discovery and transformation together. We'll explore ideas that challenge our current thinking and open up new horizons. This is about envisioning a world where technology doesn't just change our lives; it becomes a part of who we are, redefining the human experience in unimaginable ways.

This exploration is more than an academic exercise; it's a participatory odyssey into the heart of what could be humanity's most significant milestone. We stand on the threshold of a future where the lines between human and machine, biology and technology, reality and possibility merge.

MOORE'S LAW

Moore's law is a principle that has profoundly influenced our understanding of technological growth. Coined by Gordon Moore, co-founder of Intel, Moore's law predicts that the number of transistors on a microchip doubles approximately every two years while the cost of computers drastically decreases. This law, more of an observation, has held true for decades and has become a cornerstone in predicting technological advancement.

To fully grasp the impact of Moore's law, consider the allegory of the chessboard, often recounted in discussions of exponential growth. It's a story that illustrates our difficulty in comprehending the power of doubling, a concept central to Moore's law. The tale speaks of a chess inventor who asks for a seemingly modest reward—grains of rice, doubled on each square of the chessboard. What starts as a simple request escalates into an immense number, exceeding the rice production of the entire world. This story parallels the growth we've witnessed in technology—what seems modest at first escalates exponentially, leading to massive advancements.

This phenomenon isn't just theoretical; it's evident in the evolution of computers and smartphones. Early computers filled entire rooms, yet today's smartphones, far more powerful, fit in our palms. This exponential improvement isn't limited to computing power; it also extends to storage capacity, network speeds, and even the resolution of digital cameras.

As we enter what some call the "second half of the chessboard" in technological advancement, the effects of Moore's law become even more pronounced and unpredictable. We're reaching a point where the leaps in capability are so vast, they're difficult to comprehend. This is the era where artificial intelligence, quantum computing, and biotechnology are not just improving incrementally but are advancing at a pace that could soon surpass human understanding.

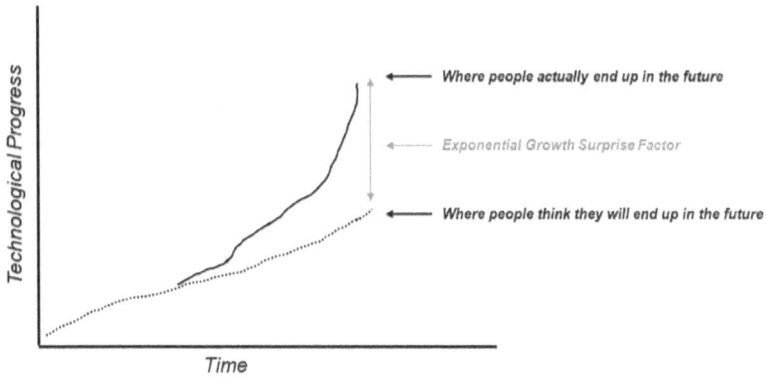

But Moore's law is more than just a predictor of technological growth; it's a catalyst for innovation. It drives companies to aim for ambitious goals, knowing that what seems impossible today might be feasible tomorrow. It's a reminder that boundaries in technology are constantly being pushed, leading to breakthroughs that were once the realm of science fiction.

Yet, as with all exponential growth, Moore's law faces its limits. As we approach the physical limitations of silicon-based technology, there's a growing discussion about what comes next. Will new materials or quantum computing take over, continuing the trend Moore observed? Or will we see a slowdown in the pace of technological advancement?

Ray Kurzweil developed the "Law of Accelerating Returns" concept, which can be seen as an extension of Moore's law. He argues that technological progress, particularly in information technologies, follows an exponential rather than a linear trajectory. This means that the rate of change itself is accelerating, leading to profound and rapid transformations in society. For Kurzweil, Moore's law is not just about the increasing power of computers; it's a signpost of a broader trend towards more advanced, efficient, and compact technologies in all fields.

EMBRACING SINGULARITY

In Chapter 9, we embarked on a journey to understand Universal Intelligence, a concept in which human knowledge is no longer fragmented, leading to a more complete and harmonious understanding of our world. Chapter 10 explores the "empathic revolution," highlighting the use of technology as a tool for self-understanding, social awareness, and deliberate learning, enabling deeper human connections, fostering a world rich in compassion and mutual respect. In Chapter 11, we ventured into the realm of potential immortality through technological means, leaving our mark in this world beyond the physical. The pattern here is clear: each chapter methodically builds upon the last, expanding our understanding from the broad conceptualization of intelligence to its application in fostering human connection, and finally, to overcoming human limits altogether. This progression not only reinforces the continuity of the book but also illustrates the building-block nature of our approach to Singularity. By grasping these concepts, you are not only following the logical sequencing of ideas but also preparing to envision the possibilities of Singularity, although the exact details are left to your imagination.

Imagine a world where opening an app on your smartphone to make a transaction is replaced by the effortless power of your mind. So, instead, you do it instantly through actioning a thought. This isn't Singularity yet, but it's a very small step in that direction. This example aligns more closely with transhumanism, a philosophy that embraces technology to enhance human abilities and overcome physical limitations. Of course, with such advancements come concerns. Some might worry about security breaches, where someone could manipulate your thoughts. Let me emphasize security and privacy protections will evolve in tandem with our technological advancements. History offers us a roadmap, reassuring us that safeguards will keep pace with innovation. Ultimately, it's our choice, whether we retreat in fear or forge ahead towards the potential.

The question we face is not just about how we employ technology and how we secure it, but how we infuse it with our human values.

Drawing inspiration from Brynjolfsson and McAfee's optimism yet charting an independent path, I envision a future where technology is an enabler of dreams, a nurturer of potentials, and a catalyst for a more inclusive and compassionate world. This is a future where our innovations reflect our deepest human values, where every leap in technology is matched by a leap in our capacity for empathy and understanding.

In shaping this future, the responsibility lies not just with the technologists and innovators but with each one of us as Brynjolfsson and McAfee highlight. Every choice we make, every technology we embrace, is a step towards the future we aspire to create. This journey is about harnessing the power of technology to build a world that resonates with the harmony of human values, a world where every individual can thrive, not just survive. As we navigate the second machine age, our focus shifts from mere survival and economic prosperity to seeking fulfillment in creativity, community, and connection. The true promise of this era is not just in unleashing technological potential but in unlocking the reservoirs of human creativity and compassion. The technologies we create are not ends in themselves but keys that unlock doors to new realms of possibility.

GETTING CLOSER TO SINGULARITY

Ray Kurzweil offers a fascinating perspective on the trajectory of technological evolution. He posits that its fundamental drive is towards increasing complexity and intelligence, mirroring attributes often ascribed to the divine:

> [Technology] Evolution moves toward greater complexity, greater elegance, greater knowledge, greater intelligence, greater beauty, greater creativity, and greater levels of subtle attributes such as love. In every monotheistic tradition God is likewise described as all of these qualities, only without any limitation: infinite knowledge, infinite intelligence, infinite beauty, infinite creativity, infinite love, and so on.[1]

While the evolution of technology may never reach true infinity in these qualities, its exponential acceleration propels it ever closer to that ideal.

Singularity is a tricky thing to think about. For me, it's like trying to understand something as deep and hard to explain as the soul. We know it's there, but it's tough to put into words. Ray Kurzweil said it's like trying to look directly at the sun—it's too bright and hard to focus on. That's a good way to describe how challenging it is to think about Singularity.

MOTIVES AND CHALLENGES DRIVING US TOWARDS SINGULARITY

Ray Kurzweil's provocative ideas about the accelerating pace of technological progress have inspired my own thinking about humanity's evolution towards Singularity. Drawing from his perspective, I see several key issues that motivate us as human to transcend our limitations:

- *Body Issues*: our biological bodies are not well-suited to the current environment, as they operate under obsolete genetic programs. Ray Kurzweil states, "Our bodies are governed by obsolete genetic programs that evolved in a bygone era, so we need to overcome our genetic heritage. We already have the knowledge to begin to accomplish this, something I am committed to doing."[2] This is his perspective on the necessity of transcending our genetic constraints. Imagine a future where aging isn't a one-way street. Science is cracking the code on life, revealing it's not a matter of simply getting older, but rather a collection of challenges we can potentially overcome. This opens doors to incredible possibilities—tools inspired by biology that could help us live longer, healthier lives. These concepts and principles are extensions of the discussions initiated in Chapters 8 and 11.

- *Death Issues*: I view death as a significant loss of a unique pattern of knowledge and experience. Each person represents a complex pattern, and their loss signifies the disappearance of irreplaceable information. Currently, we lack the means to fully preserve or back up this unique pattern. This perspective highlights the importance of each individual's unique contribution to collective human knowledge. As Kurzweil emphasizes, "Knowledge is precious in all its forms: music, art, science, and technology, as well as the embedded knowledge in our bodies and brains. Any loss of this knowledge is tragic."[3] That's why in Chapter 9, we propose the concept of Universal Intelligence, aiming to ensure that human knowledge is no longer fragmented or lost, leading to a more complete and harmonious understanding of our world and humanity.

- *War Issues*: war is tragically impactful, particularly for those who have no say in the decisions made by their leaders. Beyond the immediate casualties, war inflicts deep wounds on society. It destroys irreplaceable knowledge, dismantles cultural heritage, and leaves a lasting scar on the collective psyche. Albert Einstein poignantly highlighted the severe consequences of such conflicts when he speculated, "I know not with what weapons World War III will be fought, but World War IV will be fought with sticks and stones." This statement underscores the regression and devastation that could follow from modern warfare, stripping humanity of its advancements and thrusting it back into primitive conditions.

In my view, war represents one of humanity's greatest losses, primarily driven by the egos of politicians. In Chapter 10, I discussed the concept of an "empathy revolution through technology" as a potential solution. Historical analysis shows that many conflicts and wars have been triggered by misunderstandings and misinformation. Many of the most destructive wars stemmed from a chain reaction of mistrust and misinterpretations between nations. Therefore, the key to preventing future wars lies in cultivating greater empathy enabled through AI.

How I Envision Singularity

Everyone holds their unique vision and imagination of Singularity, and there are no definitive right or wrong answers. For philosopher and futurist Max More, Singularitarianism is not a system of beliefs or unified viewpoints: "While it is fundamentally an understanding of basic technology trends, it is simultaneously an insight that causes one to rethink everything, from the nature of health and wealth to the nature of death and self."[4] For Kurzweil, Singularity may not achieve infinite levels of computation, memory, or other measurable attributes, but it certainly reaches vast levels of all these qualities, including intelligence. He suggests that by reverse-engineering the human brain, we could harness its complex, self-organizing patterns within powerful computers. This advanced form of intelligence could then continuously upgrade itself, rapidly improving both its hardware and software components. As roboticist, author, and robotics entrepreneur, Rodney Brooks states, "Our machines will become much more like us, and we will become much more like our machines."[5]

Here, I offer my own perspective on Singularity. This is not a proposal for new doctrine, but rather a reflection of my imagination and how I envision it:

- *Mind-Blowing New Intelligence*: beyond our current comprehension, a new form of intelligence will emerge. It's a type of awareness that goes beyond our current scope, pushing the boundaries of what we consider possible. This intelligence isn't just about knowledge or cognitive ability; it's about understanding the universe and our place within it in a completely new way.
- *Energetic Intelligence*: I imagine my intelligence as a dynamic energy. It's not confined by physical limits but can traverse barriers like walls and move as swiftly as light. This intelligence is capable of interacting with other intelligent entities, whether they are human souls or different forms of life and energy.
- *Harmonious Intelligence*: In Singularity, I foresee a state where my intelligence seamlessly integrates with my body and soul. This profound unity allows me to fully comprehend and connect with my soul on a conscious level through my intelligence, merging the very core of my being with the enhanced capacities of my mind. This concept echoes neuroscientist Giulio Giorelli's intriguing assertion, "Yes, we have a soul. But it's made of lots of tiny robots."[6] Giorelli's statement suggests that what we consider our soul might actually be comprised of countless small, interconnected components or intelligent systems working in harmony.
- *Cosmic Communication and Travel*: Singularity enables my soul to journey across the cosmos, engaging with diverse life forms and energies. Communication in this state transcends traditional language; it's an intuitive exchange of action and reaction, akin to the interplay of energies. This form of communication is intrinsic, a natural interaction where understanding is immediate and profound.
- *Unlimited Time*: I foresee a transformation where time, as we experience it, becomes a boundless resource. Technology

liberates us from the constraints of mundane tasks, ushering in an era where time stretches infinitely before us. This new expanse of time allows us to engage more deeply with our passions or to immerse ourselves in the pure joy of existence. Within this limitless temporality, our choices about how to spend our time become reflections of our true selves, enabling a life lived with unprecedented intention and freedom.

In this vision of Singularity, my understanding of intelligence, energy, and existence evolves dramatically. It's a future where the boundaries between knowledge, consciousness, and the physical world become fluid, allowing for experiences and interactions that are currently beyond our wildest imaginations. Singularity, as I see it, isn't just a technological milestone; it's a transformative leap in our very essence as beings, opening doors to realms of understanding and capabilities that redefine what it means to be human. In this context, the idea of "born dead—die alive" profoundly resonates, as it encapsulates the journey from a predetermined biological existence to a dynamically redefined life through technology—where we are born into a limited physical form but have the potential to transcend these limitations and truly come alive in ways we are only beginning to comprehend.

CHAPTER 12 TAKEAWAYS

Moore's law describes the doubling of transistors on computer chips roughly every two years, driving exponential growth in computing power and cost reduction. This principle of rapid, unimaginable growth has shaped the trajectory of technology for decades.

This growth isn't just about computers getting smaller and faster. It impacts everything from AI to biotechnology. We're moving into a realm where the pace of advancement could soon outpace even our ability to fully comprehend it.

Singularity is a hypothetical point where technological progress becomes so rapid and transformative that it fundamentally alters human existence. It's a concept with many interpretations, but here's one view: technology could overcome biological limitations of life and intelligence, blurring the lines between human and machine. Intelligence may evolve into something far beyond what we understand today, reshaping our perception of the universe. Communication and travel could become limitless, potentially allowing interactions with other life forms or energies across the cosmos.

This potential future raises crucial questions. For example, how do we ensure technology serves humanity, not special interests? Can we embed human empathy and compassion into these advancements? How do we preserve individual autonomy and free will in a technologically enhanced world?

Technology isn't destiny. We must shape it responsibly, ensuring it's a tool for positive change. This calls for individual choices and a collective focus on using technology to build a future where everyone thrives, a true "Second Machine Age" where human creativity and compassion are amplified, not replaced.

Moore's Law shows just how fast technology can change. Singularity is a reminder that the future isn't pre-determined. We have the power and responsibility to create a world where technological progress works in harmony with our deepest human values.

FINAL WORDS

As we conclude this journey, it is evident that people today possess the tools and potential to redefine our existence. By harnessing technology responsibly and thoughtfully, we can transition from being "born dead" to truly "dying alive," living lives that transcend the limitations of our physical existence. This book is a call to action to embrace the transformative power of technology, not just for entertainment or superficial gains, but to fundamentally improve the human condition.

Let us envision a future where technology enhances our lives, extends our lifespans, and fosters a deeper sense of connection and purpose. Let us work towards a world where we are not merely surviving, but truly living—continuously evolving and thriving in ways once unimaginable. The journey from "born dead" to "die alive" is not just a personal transformation, but a societal one, where we collectively redefine what it means to be human in the age of technology.

By integrating these insights and reflections, we can shape a future where technological advancements are harnessed to enhance humanity, promoting a life that is richer, more connected, and infinitely more meaningful.

ACKNOWLEDGMENTS

To my mom, thank you for nurturing my drive to pursue my dreams— your unwavering belief in me has given me the courage to keep reaching for the stars. You were my teacher, coach, and a veritable compass, always guiding me in the right direction.

To my dad, thank you for always believing in me—your unwavering support fueled my ambition, and your "yes" to my crazy ideas instilled in me a love for learning that continues to guide me.

To my sisters, my lifelong companions, and biggest cheerleaders—you've always been there to listen, support, and celebrate my milestones. Thank you for being a constant source of strength and joy.

A heartfelt thank you to all the friends who cheered me on and never doubted me, even when things got tough.

To my editor, Nancy Pile—your invaluable contributions to this book have made it possible. Your expertise and guidance have been instrumental in bringing this project to life.

And to the inspiring authors like Hal Elrod, whose work has profoundly impacted my life and discipline—thank you for being an example. Your words have made a difference.

NOTES

Introduction—The Quest Begins

[1] Ray Kurzweil, *The Singularity Is Near: When Humans Transcend Biology* (New York: Viking, 2005).

[2] Erik Brynjolfsson and Andrew McAfee, *The Second Machine Age* (New York: WW Norton, 2016).

[3] Aaron Garrison, "Mind, Machine, and the Empathic Revolution: Manifesto for a New World" (CreateSpace Independent Publishing Platform, 2016).

Chapter 1: Technology's Dance: Directed by Society, Politics and Economy

[1] Mariam Suboh, "NEOM'S The Line: The World's First Cognitive City," WIRED, August 11, 2020, https://wired.me/technology/neoms-the-line-the-worlds-first-cognitive-city/.

Chapter 2: Unifying Digital Realms: Individual Actions, Systemic Solutions

[1] Susan Schneegans, Jake Lewis, and Tiffany Straza, eds. "UNESCO Science Report: The Race against Time for Smarter Development; Executive Summary," United Nations Educational, Scientific and Cultural Organization, 2021, https://unesdoc.unesco.org/ark:/48223/pf0000377250.

[2] Ibid.

Chapter 3: Unveiling the "True" Value

[1] "Clarke's Three Laws," Wikipedia, last modified April 4, 2024, accessed May 6, 2024, https://en.wikipedia.org/wiki/Clarke%27s_three_laws.

2   George W. Burns, "Gross National Happiness: A Gift from Bhutan to the World" in *Positive Psychology as Social Change*, ed. Robert Biswas-Diener (New York: Springer, 2011), 73–87.

3   "Urban Development Overview," World Bank, April 3, 2023, https://www.worldbank.org/en/topic/urbandevelopment/overview.

4   "World Cities Report 2020," United Nations Human Settlements Programme, 2020, https://unhabitat.org/sites/default/files/2020/10/wcr_2020_report.pdf.

5   Avik Roy, "Key Findings from the 2022 World Index of Healthcare Innovation," FREOPP.org, March 16, 2023, https://freopp.org/key-findings-from-the-2022-world-index-of-healthcare-innovation-e2a772f55b92.

6   "New Report Shows Growth in Federal and Private Sector Medical R&D Investment," Research America, February 9, 2022, https://www.researchamerica.org/press-releases-statements/new-report-shows-growth-in-federal-and-private-sector-medical-rd-investment/.

7   Mauro Giuffè and Dennis L. Shung, "Harnessing the Power of Synthetic Data in Healthcare: Innovation, Application, and Privacy," *npj Digital Medicine* 6, no. 186 (2023), https://doi.org/10.1038/s41746-023-00927-3

8   William D. Nordhaus, "The Health of Nations: The Contribution of Improved Health to Living Standards," in *Measuring the Gains from Medical Research: An Economic Approach*, eds. Kevin M. Murphy and Robert H. Topel (Chicago: University of Chicago Press, 2003) 9–40, https://doi.org/10.7208/9780226551791-002.

9   Kevin M. Murphy and Robert H. Topel, "The Value of Health and Longevity," *Journal of Political Economy* vol. 114, no. 5 (October 2006): 871–904, https://doi.org/10.1086/508033.

10 Andrea Downey, "DeepMind's Streams App Saves £2,000 per Patient, Peer Review Finds," Digital Health, July 31, 2019, https://www.digitalhealth.net/2019/07/deepminds-streams-saves-2000-peer-review/; A. Connell et al., "Implementation of a Digitally Enabled Care Pathway (Part 1): Impact on Clinical Outcomes and Associated Health Care Costs," *Journal of Medical Internet Research* 21, no. 7 (July 15, 2019): e13147, doi: 10.2196/13147.

Chapter 4: The Subtle Art of Algorithmic Influence

1   "Attention Spans, Consumer Insights, Microsoft Canada," Microsoft Attention Spans, Spring 2015, https://dl.motamem.org/microsoft-attention-spans-research-report.pdf.

2   Mason Walker and Katerina Eva Matsa, "News Consumption Across Social Media in 2021," Pew Research Center, September 20, 2021, https://www.pewresearch.org/journalism/2021/09/20/news-consumption-across-social-media-in-2021/#:~:text=A%20little%20under%20half%20(48,8%2C%202021.

3   Eli Pariser, *The Filter Bubble: What the Internet Is Hiding from You* (New York: Penguin Press, 2011).

4   U. Agudo and H. Matute, "The Influence of Algorithms on Political and Dating Decisions," *PLoS One* 16, no. 4 (April 21, 2021): e0249454, doi: 10.1371/journal.pone.0249454.

5   "The Social Dilemma: Social Media and Your Mental Health," Mass General Brigham McLean, March 29, 2024, https://www.mcleanhospital.org/essential/it-or-not-social-medias-affecting-your-mental-health.

6   "Study: False News Spreads Faster Than the Truth," MIT Management Sloan School, March 8, 2018, https://mitsloan.mit.edu/ideas-made-to-matter/study-false-news-spreads-faster-truth.

7   "2023 Gen Z and Millennial Survey," Deloitte, accessed April 17, 2023, https://www2.deloitte.com/content/dam/Deloitte/si/Documents/deloitte-2023-genz-millennial-survey.pdf.

Chapter 6: Echoes of Generations: From Digital Divide to Digital Harmony

1   Serah Louis, "Here's the Average Salary Each Generation Says It Needs to Feel 'Financially Healthy.' Gen Z Requires a Whopping $171K/Year—What Salary Do You Need to Feel Secure?" Yahoo! Finance, June 30, 2023, https://finance.yahoo.com/news/heres-average-salary-generation-says-140000949.html#.

2   Rosalie Macmillan, "Gen Z at Work: Embracing Change & Driving Innovation," Flair HR, August 23, 2023, https://flair.hr/en/blog/gen-z-at-work/.

3   Ibid.

4   "2023 Gen Z and Millennial Survey," Deloitte, accessed April 17, 2024, https://www2.deloitte.com/content/dam/Deloitte/si/Documents/deloitte-2023-genz-millennial-survey.pdf.

5   "Report Finds Americans Willing to Pay More for Sustainable Products," PDI Technologies, April 26, 2023, https://pditechnologies.com/news/consumers-willing-pay-more-sustainability/.

6   Krismary Sharmaine Yapo, "How the Entry of Generation Z Reshape the Workforce," LinkedIn, October 23, 2023, https://www.linkedin.com/pulse/how-entry-generation-z-reshape-workforce-krismary-sharmaine-yapo/.

7   "Gen Z Travelers: More Open to Influence and Inspiration than Other Generations," Expedia Group Media Solutions, November 14, 2018, https://advertising.expedia.com/about/press-releases/gen-z-travelers-more-open-to-influence-and-inspiration-than-other-generations/.

8   "Spirituality Among Americans," Pew Research Center, December 7, 2023, https://www.pewresearch.org/religion/2023/12/07/spirituality-among-americans/.

Chapter 7: The IQ Era Ends: Building the Augmented Human Intelligence

1. Adeel Ahmed et al., "Spiritual Intelligence (SQ): A Holistic Framework for Human Resource Development," *Revista Administratie Si Management Public,* Faculty of Administration and Public Management, Academy of Economic Studies, Bucharest, Romania, no. 26 (2016): 60–77; James L. Gould and Carol Grant Gould, *The Animal Mind* (New York: Scientific American Library, 1994).

2. S. Kermarrec et al., "Anxiety Disorders in Children with High Intellectual Potential," *BJPsych Open* 6, no. 4 (July 6, 2020): e70, doi: 10.1192/bjo.2019.104.

3. Ibid.

4. Kristin Samuelson, "Americans' IQ Scores Are Lower in Some Areas, Higher in One," Northwestern Now, March 20, 2023, https://news.northwestern.edu/stories/2023/03/americans-iq-scores-are-lower-in-some-areas-higher-in-one/#:~:text=IQ%20scores%20have%20substantially%20increased,as%20the%20%E2%80%9CFlynn%20effect.%E2%80%9D.

5. Evan Horowitz, "IQ Rates Are Dropping in Many Developed Countries and That Doesn't Bode Well for Humanity," NBC News, May 22, 2019, https://www.nbcnews.com/think/opinion/iq-rates-are-dropping-many-developed-countries-doesn-t-bode-ncna1008576.

6. Ulric Neisser et al., "Intelligence: Known and Unknowns," *American Psychologist* 51, no. 2 (1996): 77–101, doi:10.1037//0003-066X.51.2.77.

7. C. Chiu, Y. Hong, and C. S. Dweck, "Toward an Integrative Model of Personality and Intelligence: A General Framework and Some Preliminary Steps," in *Personality and Intelligence,* eds. R. J. Sternberg and P. Ruzgis (New York: Cambridge University Press), 104–134.

8. R. A. Emmons, "Is Spirituality an Intelligence? Motivation, Cognition, and the Psychology of Ultimate Concern," *The International Journal for the Psychology of Religion* 10, no. 1 (2000): 3–26, doi:10.1207/S15327582IJPR1001_2.

9. Stuart J. Ritchie and Elliot Tucker-Drob, "How Much Does Education Improve Intelligence? A Meta-Analysis," *Psychological Science* 29, no. 8 (June 2018), doi: 10.1177/0956797618774253.

10. Sandie Gay, Michelle Bishop and Stuart Sutherland, "Teaching Genetics and Genomics for Social and Lay Professionals," in *Genomics and Society Ethical, Legal, Cultural and Socioeconomic Implications,* eds. Dhavendra Kumar and Ruth Chadwick, (Cambridge, Massachusetts: Academic Press, 2016), 147–164.

11. "Health Advisory on Social Media Use in Adolescence," American Psychological Association, May 2023, https://www.apa.org/topics/social-media-internet/health-advisory-adolescent-social-media-use?_ga=2.155969723.1881775648.1706544591-1807171316.1704824919; Heather Stringer, "Generations Unite to Address Loneliness, Climate Change, Other

Global Challenges," American Psychological Association, March 1, 2024, https://www.apa.org/monitor/2024/03/generations-connect-loneliness-climate-change#:~:text=URL%3A%20https%3A%2F%2Fwww.apa.org%2Fmonitor%2F2024%2F03%2Fgenerations,100.

12 Helen Vossen and Patti M. Valkenburg, "Do Social Media Foster or Curtail Adolescents' Empathy? A Longitudinal Study," *Computers in Human Behavior* no. 63 (October 2016): 118–124, doi:10.1016/j.chb.2016.05.040.

13 Y. Chen and Y. Xu, "Exploring the Effect of Social Support and Empathy on User Engagement in Online Mental Health Communities," *International Journal of Environmental Research and Public Health* 18, no. 13 (June 26, 2021): 6855, doi: 10.3390/ijerph18136855.

14 Yonty Friesem, "Developing Digital Empathy," in *Advances in Media, Entertainment, and the Arts*, ed. Giuseppe Amoruso (Hershey, Pennsylvania: IGI Global, 2016), 45–160.

15 "What Does the Research Say? Hundreds of Independent Studies Confirm: SEL Benefits Students," CASEL, accessed May 23, 2024, https://casel.org/fundamentals-of-sel/what-does-the-research-say/.

16 C. Miller-Perrin and E. K. Mancuso, *Faith from a Positive Psychology Perspective* (New York: Springer, 2014).

17 M. R. Taghizadeh Yazdi, "Quantitative Assessment of Spiritual Capital in Changing Organizations by Principal Component Analysis and Fuzzy Clustering," *Journal of Organizational Change Management* 28, no. 3 (May 2015): 469–485, doi:10.1108/JOCM-07-2014-0127.

18 "Millennials Are Less Religious Than Older Americans, but Just as Spiritual," Pew Research Center, November 23, 2015, https://www.pewresearch.org/short-reads/2015/11/23/millennials-are-less-religious-than-older-americans-but-just-as-spiritual/#:~:text=Just%2027%25%20of%20Millennials%20say,with%20those%20in%20older%20generations.

19 "What Role Do Religion and Spirituality Play in Mental Health?" American Psychological Association, 2013, https://www.apa.org/news/press/releases/2013/03/religion-spirituality.

20 Graham Rossiter, "The Spiritual and Moral Dimension to the School Curriculum: A Perspective on Across-the-Curriculum Studies," January 2009, doi:10.1007/1-4020-5246-4_48; Ira C. Lupu, F. Elwood, and Eleanor Davis, "Religion in the Public Schools," Pew Research Center, October 3, 2019, https://www.pewresearch.org/religion/2019/10/03/religion-in-the-public-schools-2019-update/.

21 "Global Mindfulness Meditation Apps Market Outlook to 2027—A USD 4,206 Million Market by 2027—ResearchAndMarkets.com," Businesswire, March 5, 2021, https://www.businesswire.com/news/home/20210305005147/en/Global-Mindfulness-Meditation-Apps-Market-Outlook-to-2027---A-USD-4206-Million-Market-by-2027---ResearchAndMarkets.com.

22 "Social: GlobalWebIndex's Flagship Report on the Latest Trends in Social Media," GlobalWebIndex, 2020, https://www.gwi.com/hubfs/Social%20 Media%20Trends%20Report.pdf?sbrc=1gdn8hbD-aDjRiBvV1JM-hg%3D%3 D%248MqYz9TUB2uNPV6Ao0lV_w%3D%3D.

23 David DeSteno, "Is Religion Good for Health?" *Wall Street Journal*, June 8, 2023, https://www.wsj.com/articles/is-religion-good-for-your-health-921814a7.

24 A. J. Guimond et al., "Sense of Purpose in Life and Inflammation in Healthy Older Adults: A Longitudinal Study," *Psychoneuroendocrinology* no. 141 (July 2022): 105746, doi: 10.1016/j.psyneuen.2022.105746.

Chapter 8: The Quest for Human-Equivalent Computing

1 Elizabeth Nance, "Careers in Nanomedicine and Drug Delivery," *Advanced Drug Delivery Review* 144 (April 2019): 180–189, doi: 10.1016/j.addr.2019.06.009.

2 Kumar S. Ray and Mandrita Mondal, "Prediction of Radiation Fog by DNA Computing," *New Mathematics and Natural Computation* 16, no. 2 (2020): 231–254, https://doi.org/10.1142/S1793005720500143.

Chapter 9: Universal Intelligence

1 Douglas Burnham, "Gottfried Leibniz: Metaphysics," Internet Encyclopedia of Philosophy, accessed May 23, 2024, https://iep.utm.edu/leib-met/.

2 Qur'an (81:1), https://islamicstudies.info/reference.php?sura=81&verse=1-14#:~:text=(81%3A1)%20When%20the,81%3A7)%20when7%20the.

3 Jordan Peterson, *Fasting Prolongs Life by 40%*, YouTube, September 3, 2023, video, 25 seconds, https://www.youtube.com/shorts/Y8L7RJN0SoE.

4 Rachael Ajmera, "8 Health Benefits of Fasting, Backed by Science," Healthline, September 22, 2023, https://www.healthline.com/nutrition/fasting-benefits#inflammation.

Chapter 10: Empathy Reimagined Through Technology

1 M. S. Tarsha and D. Narvaez, "The Evolved Nest, Oxytocin Functioning, and Prosocial Development," *Frontiers in Psychology* no. 14, (June 22, 2023): 1113944, doi: 10.3389/fpsyg.2023.1113944.

Chapter 11: Death 2.0: Can We Live Forever?

1 Ray Kurzweil, *The Singularity Is Near: When Humans Transcend Biology* (New York: Viking, 2005).

Chapter 12: Is Singularity Near?

[1] Ray Kurzweil, *The Singularity Is Near: When Humans Transcend Biology* (New York: Viking, 2005).

[2] Ibid.

[3] Ibid.

[4] Ibid.

[5] Rodney Brooks, *Flesh and Machines: How Robots Will Change Us* (New York: Pantheon, 2002).

[6] Daniel C. Dennett, *Freedom Evolves* (New York: Viking, 2003).

AUTHOR BIO

Salma NOUN, a Business Strategy Advisor to government executives and private companies, is a passionate advocate for emerging technologies. She leverages her expertise in fostering economic development and technological advancement, in conjunction with her captivating public speaking and writing skills, to raise awareness and influence leadership perspectives. Her robust background in engineering and digital management consulting fuels her passion for ensuring technology serves as a force for positive change.

Salma translates complex concepts into clear and engaging narratives. This allows her to bridge the gap between cutting-edge advancements and their real-world impact. She is a leading voice for positive change, empowering audiences and readers to embrace technology, not as a threat, but as a tool for personal growth, meaningful connections, and a brighter future.

Salma's journey as an author is just beginning. By combining her expertise with her passion for storytelling, she aims to become a leading voice for positive change in a world increasingly shaped by technology.

Her core reason for writing is to empower individuals to embrace technology's potential for good. Salma aims to dispel the prevailing negative mindset that technology will bring only destruction and disconnection. Instead, she wants to show how technology can enhance our lives, lead to longevity, and foster a deeper sense of connection. By challenging misconceptions and promoting a more balanced understanding, she aspires to inspire readers to harness the transformative power of technology for personal growth, meaningful relationships, and a brighter future.

You can contact Salma NOUN for podcasting and speaking engagements at salmanoun@gmail.com.

REVIEW ASK

Thank You For Reading My Book!

I really appreciate all of your feedback and

I love hearing what you have to say.

I need your input to make the next version of this

book and my future books better.

Please take two minutes now to leave a helpful review on

Amazon letting me know what you thought of the book.

Thanks so much!

- Salma Noun

www.ingramcontent.com/pod-product-compliance
Lightning Source LLC
Chambersburg PA
CBHW030917120626
46554CB00001B/180